CHINA IN YOUR POCKET

CHINA IN YOUR POCKET

A STEP-BY-STEP GUIDE
AND TRAVEL ITINERARY

BY GAYLON DUKE
AND ZENIA VICTOR

Northcote House

British Library Cataloguing in Publication Data

Duke, Gaylon
 China in your pocket : a step-by-step guide and travel
 itinerary. — UK ed. — (Pocket travellers).
 1. China — Visitors' guides
 I. Title II. Victor, Zenia III. Duke, Gaylon. China in 22 days IV.
 Series 915.1'0458

ISBN 1-85373-016-5

© 1987 by Gaylon Duke and Zenia Victor
UK edition © 1988 by Northcote House Publishers

Maps Michael Taylor

All rights reserved. No part of this work may be reproduced, other than for the purposes of review, without the express permission of the Publishers given in writing.

This edition published in 1988 by Northcote House Publishers Ltd, Harper & Row House, Estover Road, Plymouth PL6 7PZ, United Kingdom. Tel: Plymouth (0752) 705251. Telex: 45635. Fax: (0752) 777603.

CONTENTS

How to Use This Book	7
Mei You: Getting What You Want	37
Itinerary	38
Tour 1 Hong Kong	41
Tour 2 Hong Kong — Xiamen	46
Tour 3 Xiamen	48
Tour 4 Quanzhou	53
Tour 5 Hangzhou	58
Tour 6 Shaoxing	63
Tour 7 Return to Hangzhou	65
Tour 8 Shanghai	66
Tour 9 Shanghai	71
Tour 10 Shanghai	72
Tour 11 Suzhou	74
Tour 12 Qufu	78
Tour 13 Tai Shan	81
Tour 14 Tai Shan — Beijing	83
Tour 15 Beijing	84
Tour 16 Beijing	92
Tour 17 Beijing	95
Tour 18 Beijing	100
Tours 19-20 Beijing — Hong Kong — Home	102
Itinerary Option Xian	104
Adventurers' Option Southwestern China	107
Kunming — Dali — Xishuangbanna — Huanguoshu — Shilin — Emei Shan — Leshan — Chengdu — Dazu — Tibet — Yangtze River — Guilin	
Leaving China	138
Tours to China	139
Chinese Ideograms and Number Gestures	142

China

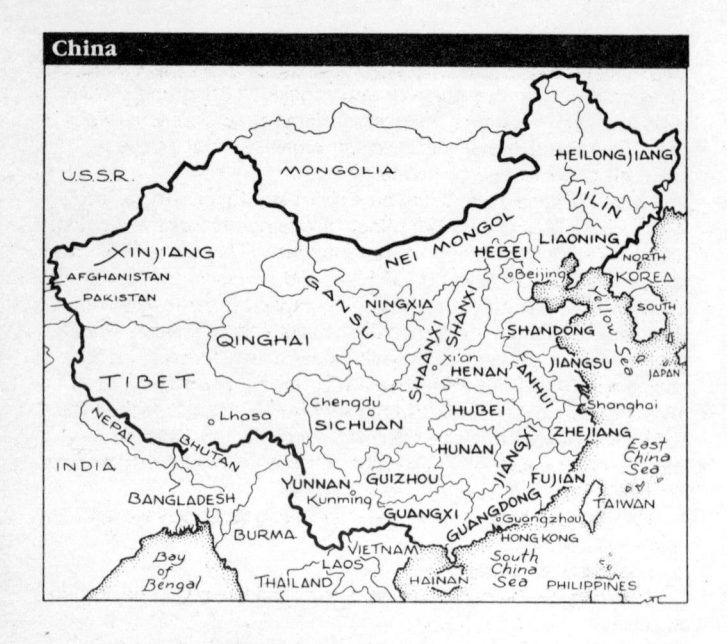

HOW TO USE THIS BOOK

This book is the tour guide in your pocket, a tried and proven plan that will show you the best of China in a few short weeks. It gives you the travel efficiency of an organised tour plus do-it-yourself freedom and flexibility.

China in Your Pocket tells you how to see China's major cities (Hangzhou, Shanghai and Beijing) and famous tourist attractions (such as the Great Wall and the Forbidden City), as well as other spots, including mystical Wuyi Shan and the sacred mountain Tai Shan which westerners rarely visit. It explains how to get there by public transport — trains, buses, boats and aeroplanes — and where to stay, eat and shop while you're there. Itinerary options are provided for those with more time; and a completely different 'Adventurers' Option' tells travellers with more flexible schedules and a willingness to trade off comfortable accommodation for unique experiences how to plunge deep into China's southwestern 'minorities' regions — all the way to Tibet.

The itinerary format we've used in this book is divided into sections, containing:

1. A **general overview**
2. A **suggested schedule** for travel, sightseeing, shopping and meals.
3. A summary of major **sightseeing highlights** (rated ●●● Don't miss; ●● Try hard to see; ● Worthwhile if you can make it), with step-by-step **walking tour** and **excursion** directions to see them.
4. **Transport** — trains, buses; boats and planes, how to book them and when to go.
5. **Food** and **lodging** recommendations.
6. Clear, user-friendly **maps**.
7. **Helpful hints**, random information titbits that will help your day go better.

Names of hotels and attractions on the map keys include corresponding Chinese characters, and in the back of the book you will find a few essential phrases written in Chinese. Point to these as needed to bridge the formidable language barrier.

Why go on your own?

If your main purpose in visiting China is to see a long list of sights, you should go with a tour group. If you wish to have the experience of being in China meeting people, finding out what is happening and how things are changing, then you should go on your own.

Travelling independently in China can be frustrating. Many procedures operate backwards: the rationality with which westerners approach tasks is often exactly opposite to the way things must be done in China. We have found through the years that whenever we use the word 'should' in contexts such as, 'The bank should be open', 'We should be able to get on that train' or 'They should still be serving dinner', we open ourselves to disillusionment. To enjoy travelling in China on your own, you'll need flexibility, patience, tolerance, and a sense of humour.

What will it cost?

The cost of travelling independently is about one-third to one-half the cost of a group tour. Your travel costs will depend on many factors. The main east coast tour from Hong Kong to Shanghai and Beijing will cost two to three times as much as a trip in southwestern or western China.

Staying in middle range hotels and not being extravagant with money, £30 ($50) a day for two people on the east coast is feasible. This would include meals, hotels, and transportation. On this same trip it would be easy to bring the cost down to about £15 ($25) a day by watching expenditure more closely and staying proportionately longer in the smaller, less expensive towns. A willingness to sleep in fairly comfortable dormitories, occasional monasteries or rooms on university campuses, take hard sleepers on trains, share boat cabins for four with the bath down the hall, and eat modest meals can bring the cost to £10 ($15) a day for two. Rock bottom is about £3 ($5) per person per day for a westerner unless you can travel as a Chinese. Chinese students can travel for a pound or two a day.

The upper limit can be whatever you are prepared to pay. Most cities now have hotels costing £60 ($100) a day. In China, however, the amount you pay often has little to do with the quality you receive. Nor do prices of most goods and services in China have any relationship to the cost of production. Prices are usually determined, as best we can work out, by someone in a Beijing back room throwing the *I Ching*.

Tour group prices, including those for mountaineering, bicycling and other adventure travel groups, work out at around £60 ($100) a day because the government sees them as an easy way to make money. Tour group organisers are not ripping off participants — they themselves have to pay inflated prices. Chinese hotels that are intended for tour groups will sometimes have extravagant room prices posted. These prices are just for show, to make tour group participants think they are getting a good deal. They can look at the price and brag to themselves, 'Wow, I'm getting a £150 ($250) a night room for only £45 ($75)'. Always keep in mind that the Chinese government encourages tourism for just one reason: to make money. Prices are adjusted to what the traffic will bear. If tourism figures show an increase, prices of all tourist services rise. If tourism seems to be dropping, prices level out. Developing competition from non-government private enterprises is becoming a major factor in keeping prices down.

Where we give prices in this book for rooms and transportation, we have taken what they were when the information was gathered (most recently in the autumn of 1986) and increased them enough to anticipate 1988 adjustments. However, nothing can allow for some increases. One guidebook took us to a hotel dormitory in Hangzhou that was listed for about 50p a night. We showed up a couple of years later and the cheapest price there was £85 ($150) a night. Price increases of this magnitude cannot be anticipated.

Hong Kong should cost about £45 ($75) a day for two. It is possible to bring the cost down to £15 ($25) a day; it's also easy to spend a fortune if you don't watch it.

There are a number of airlines flying to Hong Kong from the UK, and a number of ways of getting there, including stopovers along the way. There is also a wide range of prices. Two people spending three weeks in Hong Kong and China could reasonably expect to spend no more than £1,430 ($2,500) including the cost of getting there. It wouldn't be hard to cut the price to £1,145 ($2,000). The major part of the cost is the airfare, so longer stays cost only a fraction more than short ones.

Visas and permits

Permits to visit closed areas are rarely required, because there are almost no closed areas left. Foreigners are allowed to roam freely over most of China as long as they stay away from sensitive border zones, nuclear test sites, prison camps, and the few areas that still have not been opened due to lack of facilities.

In some parts of China, Xishuangbanna for example, permits may be required at certain times of the year to restrict the numbers of people going there, since facilities are very limited.

In 1986 the length of the tourist visa was increased to 90 days with little provision made for extensions. Word moves slowly among Chinese officials, so make sure that your initial visa is long enough to cover your stay. Emergency extensions can be obtained if needed by showing airline tickets and reservations for the near future. They know they can't get rid of you any sooner.

Where foreigners are concerned, China is not a police state. If a tourist runs foul of the law, the usual punishment is to be escorted to the border perhaps after signing a letter of self-criticism and paying a fine. It's very unlikely that you will ever have to worry about action like this. Until now China has attracted an orderly type of traveller. The opening of the border between Nepal and Tibet now brings some undesirable westerners (ie, 'druggies') north from India and Nepal. Everyone is waiting to see how the Chinese government will react. Rumour has it that this border may eventually be closed to individual travellers to eliminate the problem.

Visas can be obtained readily at numerous locations in Hong Kong within one working day. (Weekends are not working days.)

In early 1987 China announced that special provisions must be made with China International Travel Service (CITS) in Beijing to ensure accommodation before travelling to Tibet or Xinjiang. Also in early 1987 it was announced that individual tourist visas for travel in China during the peak season (May, August, September and October) can only be obtained with a letter or telex from a host organisation in China. In other months there are no problems. These short-term measures, created to cut down on overcrowding, are probably not permanent.

People who have spent time in China know that there are ways around any problem. One of those ways which was on the increase in 1987 was open solicitation of bribes by some officials and hints from others. *Never* initiate the offering of a bribe!

If your visa request is turned down for any reason, its just the beginning. Submit the request through other offices. Change the information on your form to fit what they want. Find someone who has just come back and ask how they did it. Read the 'Getting What You Want (Mei You)' section in this book, which applies to Chinese officials as well as hotel staff.

Getting to China

Numerous airlines fly to both Hong Kong and mainland China, but fares to Hong Kong can be as little as half of what it would cost to fly direct to Shanghai or Beijing.

Buying tickets through discount ticket agencies or 'bucket shops' (agencies that purchase large numbers of tickets for resale), you can get a return ticket to Hong Kong for considerably less than the normal fare, if you are prepared to put up with some inconvenience. Several airlines offer this facility. It is quite a good idea to arrange things so that you arrive in Hong Kong in the morning. If you have reserved your boat or plane into China and have your visa, you can connect directly with your ongoing transportation.

You can locate 'bucket shops' by looking at the small ads in the travel section of major newspapers. It is as well to ensure that your 'bucket shop' is reputable, and belongs to one of the recognised trade organisations.

If you have an extended time period for exploring, consider buying a one-way ticket to Hong Kong and coming back a different way. The Trans-Siberian Railway offers a route to Europe with an adventure in the process. Discount travel agents in Hong Kong, Bangkok, Penang, and Singapore can offer you interesting

How to Use This Book

fares and options on coming back. You can go overland from Tibet to Nepal and come back through India, Burma, Thailand and Singapore. At times there are good buys on tickets through Hong Kong Student Travel (you don't need to be a student) with Royal Nepal Airlines going to Hong Kong, Kathmandu, a couple of flights in Nepal, and back to Singapore.

The trips in this book are designed so that transportation from Hong Kong into and out of China can be taken care of ahead of time. To accomplish this you have to deal through a knowledgeable travel agent at home.

Be forewarned that any transportation or hotel reservations made through an agent beforehand will cost around twice the price of making the same arrangements on your own when you get to Hong Kong; but making them in Hong Kong may mean waiting for several days before you enter China. Once in China, you can make travel arrangements yourself and choose your own hotels.

Some tour organisers will make all the arrangements for individual travellers in China. The procedures are complicated and various things can go wrong, so many organisers have stopped offering this service. Those who still do are described in the back of this book, and it can be worth contacting them to see if what you want to do fits in with what they offer. The time and bother saved in China could make things easier if the considerable extra cost of having them make the arrangements is worth it to you.

Any travel agent will be able to book you into Hong Kong and out through Beijing and handle some of the basic arrangements for big city hotels. They will not be oriented to making budget arrangements, and the Chinese government charges extra for advance bookings, so these services will cost an arm and a leg.

Our recommendation for this trip is that you get a return ticket to Hong Kong, and have the first day's transportation arranged, as well as a hotel for the first night. You may want to make your last day's reservation to get back to Hong Kong. Take care of all other transport and hotels yourself, and you'll save a thousand pounds or so. Try to avoid too many advance arrangements. They tie you down and tend to go wrong.

Pack and take

TRAVEL LIGHT! Except at the most expensive hotels there will be no porters or baggage handlers. Lifts often won't work, and you'll have to carry your luggage up flights of stairs. Suitcases with wheels are useless. Plan on using a suitcase that converts into a backpack. The straps should all zip up and disappear when the bag is being used as a suitcase. External pockets should be avoided as they make pilfering easy and tend to get hung on conveyor belts and luggage racks. Some convertible suitcase/backpacks have handy detachable day packs. Buy a small to medium sized bag, since the size determines how much stuff you pack into it; a large bag encourages you to take more than you need. For a three-week trip to China your total weight should be less than twenty pounds, including a small shoulder bag for a camera and other travelling kit items you want to keep with you at all times.

Clothing: Every garment should serve more than one purpose. For example, shoes should be comfortable enough for hiking and yet look appropriate for city walking. If you can look presentable — or, better still, important — you will find yourself being treated much better in China. If you can appear to be a 'very important guest', doors open even more readily. The Chinese admire simple, practical clothing; it is easy to overdress.

Dressing in layers gives you welcome flexibility. Silk underwear, because of its warmth, lightness and comfort, is where we begin for cold climates. Natural fibres though they might take longer to dry are more adaptable to temperature changes. Avoid bulky clothing at all costs. Instead of a coat or a heavy sweater, take a bodywarmer. A hat, gloves, silk scarf, and warm socks are invaluable in cold weather.

Rubber sandals are an absolute must to prevent diseases entering the body through the feet. Though most Chinese hotels provide them, we prefer to wear our own. It is safer not to go barefoot away from home.

Sleeping: On a short trip there will be no need for a sleeping bag. If you are very fastidious and plan to visit remote areas, you may want to have your own sheet between you and the furnished bedding. Take a small airline sized pillow to use in lieu of the large Chinese-style sandbags that frequently serve as pillows, or use a bodywarmer stuffed inside a small pillowcase.

Eating: A pair of plastic chopsticks that can be wiped clean should always be with you. Other helpful items are a knife for peeling fruit, a water container (either a plastic bottle or a thermos) and a drinking cup with a lid. Your food supply should consist of instant coffee, powdered milk and some nibbles that get picked up along the way. Instant noodles, peanuts, fruit and biscuits can all be purchased in China.

Incidentals: Take a pair of sunglasses if travelling in the summer or to the west. Hong Kong is a good place to get prescription sunglasses. Don't expect to find contact lens cleaner in China. Carry string to use as a clothesline for small items and a little bag of washing powder. For large items the hotel laundries are fast and inexpensive. Always have toothpicks and dental floss handy — Chinese food gets caught between teeth. Eye masks such as those given out on airlines will come in handy at times.

Chinese cities and trains are extremely noisy by western standards so be sure to take ear plugs or you will find yourself resorting to wadded paper. For train travel a small towel, which can be purchased in China, will be handy. Though Chinese toilet paper is improving, a roll from home will be welcome. Tampons are now being manufactured in China, but you cannot count on their being available when needed.

And of course, it is a rare traveller who would feel properly equipped without his camera and film.

Medications: We wouldn't travel without antibacterial ointment, plasters, antiacid, aspirin, charcoal tablets, prescription drugs, multiple vitamins, a small container of hydrogen peroxide and another of baking powder for insect bites, and mosquito repellent for tropical areas.

Travelling Kit: Some of these items are essential to keep handy during long distance bus or train rides: a hand towel, tea cup with a lid, water container, and chopsticks. A good set of earplugs can mean the difference between comfort and permanent hearing loss. Toilet paper. A plastic vial with an aspirin, charcoal tablet, toothpick, vitamin, antiacid, etc, will save lots of rummaging.

What's the weather like?

China's vast size and geographic variety means a wide range of weather conditions will influence your travel plans.

Nothing can be more unpleasant than trying to fight China's adverse weather. Travelling along the eastern coast during the peak summer high-temperature high-humidity climate forces visitors to spend all their time and energy just trying to survive, at the expense of all the things they came to China to see and do.

Beijing in February and March, with its winds and frigid temperatures, keeps one inside and away from the Great Wall, the gardens, Forbidden City and all the other marvellous places that make Beijing interesting. And boating down the Yangtze River with the outside temperature so cold and the mist so thick that all you can do for four days is huddle in your cabin and try to keep from freezing is not quite what you imagined while planning your trip.

The Chinese use the Yangtze River as the official demarcation line showing where the weather is considered cold enough for indoor heat. North of the river public buildings (meaning most hotels) will have heating in the winter. South of the river buildings will seldom have any facilities for heating. Don't be misled by latitude — it can still get downright cold. On one of our early trips to Guangzhou (Canton) in January 1980 we *froze*. A winter blast out of Siberia made that subtropical city one of the coldest places we have ever stayed in because neither we nor the buildings were prepared for the weather.

For most of China the spring and autumn are the best times to visit. The best summer areas would be western Yunnan, western Sichuan, Tibet, Qinghai, Inner Mongolia, Beijing, and the Northeast. A midwinter trip would be most comfortable in the provinces of Guangdong, Hainan, Guangxi, Guizhou, Yunnan, and the coastal areas as far north as Shanghai. Beijing, though cold, can be clear through January.

Even though the winter days in the central part of China from Shanghai to Sichuan are not so cold, they are damp and the skies are overcast. The weather, the coal fires and the incessant hacking, spitting, and coughing lead to almost inevitable respiratory diseases. You can have absolutely marvellous experiences during this season on some of the misty sacred mountains however, as their deserted monasteries give the feeling of living inside a Chinese watercolour.

Shanghai is best in springtime because Wuxi, Suzhou's lovely gardens and the lake in Hangzhou are best seen with the trees in bloom. Bonsai displays can be seen nearly everywhere.

Health precautions

Eating and drinking offer few health problems. The Chinese system of cooking ingredients cut into small pieces over an extremely hot fire kills most germs.

We enjoy visiting markets and are generally impressed with the freshness of the food and the level of cleanliness of the market itself. (This is not true for the meat sections in a couple of smaller towns we mention in this book. It's a simple matter to avoid meat for a few days there.)

You'll almost never see anyone drinking water straight from the tap. Water is always boiled. Only at high altitudes is this method ineffective, due to the low boiling point of water (which means some germs may not be killed), so in places like Tibet alternative means of purifying water may be needed.

Bottled beverages may not always be safe. Hundreds of breweries and bottling factories have opened recently, and reports in the Chinese papers refer to cases of poor hygienic practices. Stick to widely known brands.

Hepatitis is on the increase, so taking and using your own chopsticks is particularly important. Gamma globulin is impossible to locate in China.

In the tropical south of China, malaria can be a problem if you get out of the major centres. For short trips most people rely on long clothing, mosquito repellent, and netting over the beds. Mosquito coils are readily available and during the high risk times they are kept burning in hotel rooms. For any extensive trip, consider taking cloroquine tablets and consult a doctor on the wisdom of taking fansidar for the cloroquine resistant strain of malaria.

Immunisations are recommended against polio, tetanus, and typhoid. If you are entering from another area of Asia where there is cholera or yellow fever you will need a certificate of immunisation at the Chinese border.

A vicious flu-like cold, prevalent in China, strikes down travellers especially in the winter. You may want to bring antibiotics from home to have available just in case. Conjunctivitis is another common problem. Prescription drops used at the first hint of trouble keep this from becoming serious.

For diarrhoea, which is almost inevitable with constant changes of food and water, we prefer taking charcoal tablets. They are available from your local health food store. We would never think of leaving on a trip without them.

Eating and drinking

Food in China is almost always well prepared with fresh ingredients. Your taste buds may not always delight in the cuisine, but it is healthy. You don't have to fear eating each bite as you do in so many countries.

Culinary excellence can be hard to find, mostly because you don't know what to order. A menu in China, albeit in English, can be quite mysterious for even the most experienced oriental gourmet. We discovered after months of unsuccessfully searching for our favourite 'hot and sour' soup that in China it was called 'two flavour soup'.

Asking the waiter to suggest a meal is not an effective strategy because their tendency is to recommend bland inoffensive dishes. But, as they see ever more westerners survive and even enjoy true local fare they are becoming more courageous in serving us. A good system is to learn one popular local or regional dish and order it, leaving the rest of the meal up to the suggestions of the waiter.

Another old standby is pointing to food in the kitchen, but this can yield unexpected results. Once Zenia thought she had ordered a soup, a tofu dish, and a vegetable. When the meal came it was a soup made with tofu and the vegetable.

Our most successful ordering is when we walk around the restaurant looking at what people are eating and asking how it is, most often in sign language. Thumbs up or thumbs down is understood. Pointing to it and telling the waiter, 'Yi yang' (the same) is usually understood. Sometimes when the whole meal looks like a winning combination we will order it all, though usually 'xiao' (small), accompanied by appropriate hand gestures.

Most hotel restaurants are good and are getting more inventive in their menus and decor, more refined in their service. Almost all restaurants, even the most expensive, still offer some reasonably priced dishes.

Local restaurants in all price ranges are divided into two categories — government and private; the former are usually dreary and uninviting. The food can be excellent, but the service is often downright offensive. Private restaurants are opening up all over and they, unlike those run by the government which have nothing to gain from more business, are friendly and attempt to create a pleasant atmosphere.

People on tours usually praise the service, quality, and quantity of their twice-daily banquets. We as individual travellers seldom rate that treatment. We have often watched with envy as the tour groups file in to find tables laden with appetisers, waiters buzzing around with drinks, ready to satisfy their every desire. In some of the smaller hotels they will serve a set meal that is a smaller version of what the tour groups are having.

Street eating is varied, tasty and unbelievably cheap. One problem is that as ever more people open stands some of their hygiene is poor. Eat early and at busy establishments. Both precautions are to ward against food having time to spoil.

Plastic chopsticks of your own are a necessity for street eating as well as at many restaurants. The wooden chopsticks, which are reused in most places, are not hygienic and can carry diseases including hepatitis. The government has frequent campaigns against wooden chopsticks and is even trying to discourage the traditional practice of eating from communal dishes. Breakfast is the most trying meal for a westerner. The Chinese fare is entirely different from ours, so when they try to cook eggs, bacon, and toast it comes out cold and greasy. We usually give up on such a breakfast and head out to the street in search of steamed buns or whatever is available.

Coffee is a disappointment in most restaurants. It is neither good not hot, and getting a refill can be as difficult as getting the first cup. We carry a big jar of instant coffee and powdered milk and have our morning coffee in our room. Nescafe can be purchased in most major hotels and Friendship Stores.

Vegetarians have a surprisingly difficult time keeping a strict diet. Often vegetable and tofu dishes are garnished with meat, usually pork. Their soups are generally made from a meat or chicken stock. Animal fat is often used as cooking oil. Someone who isn't bothered by tiny amounts of meat will do fine. There are a few excellent vegetarian restaurants, and many temples serve strict vegetarian meals.

Beverages such as water, tea, soft drinks, and beer are usually available, though perhaps not as you prefer them.

The Chinese routinely boil their drinking water. If you wander

How to Use This Book

around residential areas in the mornings or early evenings you will see children carrying two thermoses each to the neighbourhood hot water boiler. Like a scene from Dickens, water is boiled for the community over a coal furnace.

Traditionally the hotel rooms contain a thermos of hot water and teacups. You may have to provide your own tea. The thermoses are replenished twice a day at approximately 7:00 and 18:00. A pleasant new addition is that often a decanter full of cold water, left over from the thermoses is supplied.

Restaurants do not customarily serve water and if you try ordering it outside of the hotel restaurants they won't have it ready. Stay with hot tea which in many restaurants is no longer automatically served with the meal but must be ordered.

Bottled mineral water is readily available. Laoshan brand, which comes from the same springs as Qingdao beer, is particularly good.

Qingdao beer is by far the best, although it is difficult to find in many parts of China now. Its popularity has resulted in shortages in many places. The main reason for its scarcity, however, is that hundreds of towns now have their own local breweries and push their own product by stocking no other.

Usually the Chinese drink their beer at room temperature, which is okay in the winter but doesn't make for much of a thirst quencher in hot weather. Refrigerators are one of the five modernisations planned for all homes. As these become more widely distributed the taste for cold drinks will grow. Refrigerated beverages are usually found only in establishments that cater for westerners.

Soft drinks are popular, especially a gooey sweet orange. Coca-Cola is also found in the major centres and there is a sweeter version that the Chinese prefer. Fruit juice does not seem to be in the Chinese diet though they do have small cartons of passable fruit flavoured drinks.

Yogurt in China is called sour milk and comes in a small milk bottle or crockery pot or in a plastic container with a picture of an apple on it. Sometimes there is a deposit on the bottles and pots. It is quite good at any time, but it's best early in the day.

Cakes, biscuits, and ice cream are not as tasty as they appear, but they are very popular. Ice cream and ice lollies can be a significant cause of disease and stomach upsets. This is one of the major hazards of travelling in the hot and humid parts of China. The temptation to have something cold is sometimes overpowering and leads us to eat things even though they might kill us.

Eating hours are early for breakfast, lunch, and dinner. By the time you get around to thinking about something to eat it is probably too late. Though places frequented by westerners tend to keep more accommodating hours, don't take it for granted — always ask before you plan your day.

Some of the best eating will occur when you head off trying to find somewhere to get a bite. Street stalls are open until quite late in many places and you can usually find an appetising meal. We've never gone hungry in China though many a time we've not eaten where or what we wanted.

Is it safe?

As a westerner you are probably safer in China than any other country in the world. Chances are remote of anything unfortunate happening to you if you stay halfway alert and take sensible precautions.

The few pickpockets and pack slashers are in the big cities, almost always concentrated on the local bus going from the train station to the hotels. Your first hour in a strange city is when you are most vulnerable. Disorganised, distracted, rummaging through bags and wallets for maps and notes, you are highly susceptible to theft. Be extremely careful at these times.

Carrying a pack on your back inside a bus invites someone to slit it. Instead take it off and set it between your feet. Anything in a hip pocket is asking to be stolen in any country. Use inside pouches and money belts. Keep your large denomination notes separate from the rest of your money so you are not flashing them every time you buy something.

If you are injured on the street, don't expect the Chinese to become involved. It is not their way and has nothing to do with your being a foreigner. To become involved in misfortune is considered inauspicious.

Where can you stay?

You will encounter five general categories of hotels during your travels.

The first of these date back to the massive presence in China of the Russians who were there as engineers and technicians. The hotels they built for themselves were intended to create an environment as self-sufficient and isolated from local life as possible. The buildings are immense and well constructed, always set back from the road behind walls and gardens. The rooms are quite large, the furniture no-nonsense solid. The bathrooms are not luxurious but most of them still function. The hotel grounds offer not only room and board but every service a resident might need: banks, post office, tourist shops, barber shop, telephone and telegraph offices, and theatres that will seat thousands. Most large cities in China have one of these hotels, inevitably named Renmin (People's) or Friendship.

How to Use This Book

The next category of hotel was built in the 70s by the Chinese for western tourists. These are all copies of one another, built with no imagination and poor materials and workmanship. Maintenance is non-existent in these hotels and they have been falling apart since before they were completed. The windows don't work, the plumbing is a joke and the electrical wiring a nightmare.

The next group of hotels was built during the same period of time for overseas Chinese returning to visit. They are very basic, suffer from shoddy workmanship and are more like concrete army barracks than hotels. Rooms tend to be dormitories, baths public and down the hall, TV in the hall blaring at full volume. Receptionists don't really want you there because you might complain forcing them to clean up their act.

In these first three categories the toilets will probably run all night unless you turn off the water. The air conditioners have filters which have never been cleaned and are so clogged up they are totally inefficient. In the summer one of the first things we do is clean the filter. This also helps remove the stale odour of cigarette smoke from the air.

VIP hotels: There are lots of VIP guesthouses and a few hotels. You may never see them or even know they exist. But sometimes, for reasons unknown, a lucky traveller ends up staying in one.

Contemporary hotels: Many new hotels are being built as joint ventures. The Chinese furnish the land and employees, foreign firms furnish the supervision and structure. These have higher standards and will generally fit western taste. They tend to be flashier and more imaginative than earlier ones, but rarely function any better.

Winging it: Dormitories, monasteries, universities are to be found all over China. You will not be able to reserve a place at any of these, but you don't need to. The Russian hotels usually have three or four bed dormitories, though some are larger. The hotels built for westerners usually have large dormitories holding 20 or more beds with a separate room for each sex. If you are travelling alone and want to meet people these are good places to stay. In some hotels, like the Renmin in Chongqing for example, they automatically send all individual travellers to the dormitory.

We prefer to search out the monasteries, traditionally designed buildings or historic buildings. These places have a little taste and are more interesting to stay in. They may not be luxurious but the pleasure is in being there.

Hints: At less than a deluxe level of accommodation things change. China is an early rising and noisy country. If you enjoy your morning sleep, take a back room no matter how good the views from the front are. At 5 am the clanging, clashing, and banging of machinery begins with an accompaniment of squeaking and blaring horns and next door Chinese hacking and clearing their throat. Ahh ... morning.

Except for the new western hotels, the level of privacy will still be as you have heard. Stories of rooms being entered after just a quick cursory knock by the floor attendant are not fictitious.

The hot water for baths in some of the smaller places may be limited. It is wise to ask not only whether there is hot water but also at what time will it be available. If the hours are limited to once a day they tend to be in the evening around six so that the Chinese can bathe after work. As a rule the Chinese do not turn off the hot water taps when they finish with a shower or the sink, so if there is a limit to the water it runs out quickly.

If the price of a room seems too high, ask if they have some-thing less expensive. Some hotels such as the Renmin in Xian will only rent foreigners the most expensive rooms. You might be paying extra for a refrigerator or a TV that you won't use anyway.

The floor attendant seems to be in total charge of the floor. If you are going to be there for a while, make a friend of him. He is in charge of all your needs — hot or cold drinking water, towels, laundry, long distant phone calls, taking messages for you, even saving a room for you if you will be coming back to the same hotel as well as storing your baggage while you are gone. In some hotels the receptionist will give you a card with your room number on it and send you off to your floor. Once there you give the card to the floor attendant who will in turn give you the key. At times a deposit is requested for the key. Suggestion cards seem to be in every hotel room. These do seem to be read and at times changes are even made accordingly. Fill them in without being entirely negative or positive. A floor attendant who is a friend of ours doubles her income from bonuses received as a result of good comments. Hotel prices are so variable that many guidebooks don't even list them, fearing that outdated prices will create negative feelings. Prices depend on whether you are with a group or not, as well as on the season, how you book, and whether the receptionist likes you. Every time you register at a hotel in China you will be expected to fill in a card giving passport and residential information. Guests in hotels are categorised by nationality, so if you want to locate someone you must know what country they are from.

Transport

China offers — at least on paper — a multitude of ways to get from one place to another. Many of them are fraught with perils: changed schedules, delays, cancelled flights, non-existent boats. In this book we attempt to weave our way through this maze and connect some outstanding destinations with feasible trans-portation.

How to Use This Book

We have assumed that the traveller (you) has limited time and cannot wait days for a train in some out-of-the-way crossroads. A willingness on your part to pay more for transport will make more certain that your trip will go as scheduled.

Flying from Hong Kong to a city in China is much more expensive than first crossing into China to Canton (Guangzhou) and flying from there. Taking everything into consideration, however, we recommend the flights directly from and back to Hong Kong as being more reliable and entailing less hassle.

Long distance train travel has its own dilemmas. Since a growing percentage of the Chinese people can now afford to travel themselves, all classes on trains are often packed making it very difficult to get soft sleeper, hard sleeper; or even a seat unless you board the train at its point of origin. If you get off a train you must take your chances of finding something when you board another one. Since each of the trips in this book involves interrupting a train trip, onward tran travel might be less comfortable, but we feel the sights at these stops are so spectacular as to be worth the inconvenience.

Any guidebook that leads you to believe it is easy to get about in China is hopelessly out of date. A billion people are now on the move — on honeymoons, on business, taking produce to market, seeing their families, visiting sacred and historical sites, attending army manoeuvres or party meetings ...

Seldom can you get a ticket for the following day. You usually need to arrange transport several days in advance. The organisation of trips recommended in this book is predicated on the easiest possible advance arrangements at the beginning and the end, with enough time in the middle to arrange local transport on-site. Expect hitches to develop and learn to accept them as part of the trip.

Air Travel: The Chinese airline known by the acronym CAAC is not a wonderful airline. It will get you to your destination, though with more cancellations, delays, and confusion than most airlines. Buying a ticket is the most arduous part of the trip. The difficulty of this task governed to a great extent how we organised the itinerary in this book. Whenever possible, have a CITS or hotel person get your tickets for you.

CAAC is one of the most expensive airlines in the world, yet their offices look and function like third-class bus stations. The crowds in their disorganised queues are indeed discouraging. The desks marked Information or Foreigners Service Centre are usually unattended. If attendants are on duty they rarely have much useful information.

Before heading off to the CAAC office be sure to read the section in this book on **Information and Assistance** (p.32) and try the suggestions made there. If all else has failed and you must go to the CAAC office, talk to everyone you can, westerners and Chinese. Don't take anything for granted. Ask several people the same question, take a consensus, don't be discouraged. It is best that two of you go together, not only for mutual support but because there are usually two lines, one for arranging the ticket and one for paying. Both lines are long and to save time one person can wait in each line. They will ask to see your passport.

Once you get to the head of the line don't easily take 'no' for an answer. Read the **Mei you** section while waiting in the queue. As of 1986 CAAC was just beginning to get computers, so their information on seat availability is only approximate. They keep a certain number of tickets aside in case a VIP shows up. Our information has it that 6 seats are always left unsold until the last minute. More than once we have bought our ticket at the airport stand-by counter. This counter will not be marked as such, and most CAAC employees don't even know what stand-by means, but it is available at all the main airports in China. It will help to have a well-written message in Chinese to pass to the clerk behind the counter stating where and when you want to go.

There is usually a bus to the airport from the CAAC office and vice versa. These are not particularly comfortable, usually many people are standing, and the baggage comes on board with you, but they are reasonable and reliable. Of course taxis are available.

Pack your film and camera so that it does not go through the airport X-ray unit. Some of these are safe but some are not. The food at airport snack bars and restaurants is not very appetising but since most flights are delayed it will beat not eating. If the delay is very long, CAAC will pick up the tab for your meal.

Somewhere there will be a waiting room for group tours. If our plane is delayed we commandeer some good seats in an airy section and settle in where it is more comfortable. The tour guides in this section will also speak Chinese and English so they can keep you informed of the status of your flight. Let as many airline people as possible know what your destination is, with the hope that they will feel an obligation to keep a friendly eye on you.

Travelling at meal times does not guarantee a meal. If the flight is just a couple of hours long, it is more likely you will be served a fruit drink immediately and subsequent trips of the 'food cart' will bring souvenirs. So far we have received handkerchiefs, sun visors, toilet kits, key rings, thermometers, and fans all with the CAAC logo. Shortly before the plane lands

How to Use This Book

they will come by again, this time with a small box of sweets or dried fruit. On longer flights they will give you a packed lunch. We have yet to eat, or even recognise, anything in them besides good almond biscuits.

China is changing rapidly, hopefully for the better, and with internal competition, things are likely to get better aboard CAAC.

Trains: Buying a train ticket is potentially even more disagreeable than a plane ticket. Most stations are drab, dingy edifices that defy logic in their layouts.

In larger stations there is usually a window, or even in some places an office somewhere in the back, for foreigners to buy tickets. Somewhere, usually quite visible, is a booth manned by an elderly gentleman wearing a red arm band. He does not seem to have much to do and is generally more than happy to help foreigners. If he limits himself to pointing vaguely in a direction you don't understand, gently urge him to accompany you to the location he is indicating. If you do this politely he'll come along and save you much time and frustration. Should he not be available head for a back door, any back door, and go in. Make someone become responsible for you.

Once you've found the right queue, after the appropriate crowding and shoving, it is your turn at the window. In general, railway stations seem to be the last bastion of the cultural revolution attitude that deemed foreign devils unworthy of their time.

So set your smile in place, reread the **Mei you** chapter, and don't yield your place in line until you have your ticket in hand.

Hopefully you know where you are going and what train number you want. The lower the number the faster the train. It remains to decide what sort of seat you want. There are four possibilities on some of the trains: hard seat, soft seat, hard sleeper, soft sleeper.

Hard seat is generally to be avoided. Though perhaps acceptable for short day trips, most of the time they are miserable with crowded carriages, uncomfortable seats, and filthy conditions.

Soft seats are quite pleasant. Four good sized chairs, two on each side, face each other over a table. Tea is usually served though you often have to pay for it and frequently you will need to furnish your own cup.

Hard sleeper has six berths in a compartment, three on each side open to the aisle. On the aisle are two fold-down seats for daytime sitting, and during peak travel times cots are placed in the aisle at night. Each berth is supplied with a sheet, blanket, lumpy pillow and towel. In hot weather, instead of the sheet and blanket, they give a tatami mat and an oversized towel to cover yourself.

If you request the lowest berth, you control the window. However, during the day assorted people will be sitting, smoking and eating all over your bed. For this reason the middle berth will afford the most comfort.

Soft sleeper is an enclosed compartment with four berths and a small table. The toilets are at the end of the carriage and are slightly cleaner than the toilets in hard sleeper. The disadvantage of soft sleeper is that it is enclosed. If you are a non-smoker trapped with chain-smoking Chinese, it will be a long trip. Millions of workers travel free on trains so don't expect soft sleeper or soft seat necessarily to have a different class of person.

All sections of the train will have loudspeakers playing raucous noise from shortly before daylight to late at night. Ear plugs will be very handy; lacking those, wads of chewed up paper help a little. An advantage to the soft sleeper compartments is that they have switches in the room to turn off the speakers. All speakers are tinny and play at maximum volume the most unrecognisable noise you've ever heard. There is a master switch at the end of each carriage but if you turn it off the conductor will get annoyed and turn it back on. Some people have been known to sabotage the speakers.

Should you not be able to purchase a ticket for your preferred class, buy a hard seat ticket. Once the train is in the station go to carriage No. 8, where the conductor can often upgrade your ticket.

Bathrooms on trains are the usual squat Asian toilet with a communal sink for washing.

Boiled drinking water is almost always available, though it tends to run out on long crowded trips. In soft class the attendant will come around to fill the thermos provided in your compartment. It is more rare for this to happen in hard class. If no water shows up, watch the locals go by with their covered cups and follow them to locate the boiler.

There is often a restaurant car, especially on long distance journeys. The quality available varies widely. Some trains offer excellent food and almost elegant service. On others you have to battle the crowds to buy a ticket and then exchange it for dishes from the kitchen. Under these circumstances the food is generally very poor and not worth the bother. At stations along the way hawkers will be selling snacks from the platform.

We always travel with fruit, peanuts, biscuits, instant noodles, and whatever else we can find, just in case the food is unacceptable.

Do not throw your ticket away. If you are travelling by sleeper the attendant will take your ticket and give you a token in exchange; at the end of the journey he will give you back the ticket in exchange for the token. When you leave the station

How to Use This Book

there will be a bottleneck through narrow gates where a controller will check that each person has the proper ticket.

The stations will have at least one left luggage facility. If you check your bags in verify the opening hours to be certain that they will be open when you need to retrieve your bags. Checking your bags in gives you freedom of movement and greater convenience.

Stations also have soft class waiting rooms which you will want to use even though you might be travelling hard class. Your wait will be more comfortable, the attendant will inform you when and where to board the train, but most important of all you will be allowed to go to the platform before the hard seat masses. Just look lost and confused, which will probably be true, and someone will let you in. Don't let them turn you away. You are not prepared to fight the crowds on Chinese trains.

Trains depart on time and frequently arrive punctually, but allow yourself plenty of time at the stations. So much construction work is being done in China that several times we have found ourselves searching through a maze of obstacles for a way to reach our departing train.

Bus travel: Despite appearances and expectations, but stations are much better organised than are train stations or CAAC offices. Queues might be long but they move faster, since the paperwork of ticketing is less complicated and the personnel are more organised. Generally we are in and out of bus stations with our ticket in hand within 10 to 15 minutes. Most of the people involved in bus travel are friendly and helpful, and as in the train stations, there is often an elderly person with a red armband available to help.

Except for certain lines that cater for tourists, both foreign and Chinese, the condition of most Chinese buses is poor. Yet in some of the most unexpected out-of-the-way places in China we have found functioning, comfortable buses.

At some point during a long bus ride, in the middle of nowhere, the bus will stop and everyone will be required to get off. The bus will leave, but fear not — it will return. It has only gone to get petrol. We suspect that because Chinese are such careless and persistent smokers it's been wisely decided to keep them away from petrol stations.

Though buses move slowly, as does every means of transportation in China, they are a wonderful way to see the countryside. Along the way you will stop for meals, but not always in the most pleasing places. Bus drivers hoot constantly so you will find a pair of ear plugs beneficial.

Boats: Boats are by far the best way to travel in China, so we use them as often as possible. Tickets are easy, quick, and economical to purchase. The boats are well maintained, kept clean by a friendly efficient staff, and the food is generally acceptable and abundant. Some trips, like the crowded boat from Guangzhou to Wuzhou, are better skipped. Take the hydrofoil instead. Boats, like buses, do not have a surcharge for foreigners.

Transport within cities: Public buses are available and inexpensive in all cities. They tend to be slow and crowded, so use them only for short jaunts on direct routes.

If your destination is far away or requires a change of buses, opt for a taxi or a motorised rickshaw. Taxis are not expensive in large cities, though they frequently cost more in smaller towns. Most taxis do not have meters, so be sure to set the price beforehand. Regretfully, the day of the superhonest taxi driver is finished. You will be overcharged — sometimes a little, sometimes flagrantly. We find that taxi drivers become much more honest if we pull out a camera to take a picture of them.

It used to be that once you had a taxi you held on to it because few were available. Today availability depends on the area of the town. If you are near hotels, stations, or tourist attractions you will find many taxis parked or even cruising, but far from these areas it is rare to find a cab. You can get someone to call one for you. We sometimes hitch our way home from tourist sites on tour buses by looking tired, weary, lost and congenial.

Bicycle hire: The bicycle is the main means of transportation in China, and they are easy and inexpensive to hire. A deposit or your passport is usually requested. Most travellers much prefer to give money rather than their passport. We agree.

In general the Chinese are mellow, relaxed bike pushers, and vehicles, accustomed to bikes, are fairly considerate. The biggest hazard is being deafened by horns, since in China a driver is usually not responsible for an accident if he has hooted. As a result horns blare constantly.

Particularly in urban areas, the sheer number of bicycles gives one pause. People ride 10 to 20 abreast, with little room to the front, back or sides. Constant flow moves in leisurely fashion but necessitates great coordination.

A westerner on a bicycle will present a significant hazard as Chinese turn and stare, and run their own bikes into each other. Chinese always lock their bikes.

Car hire: Cars that you can drive yourself are not presently available in China. Cars with drivers can be arranged through

CITS, and in some parts of China chauffeured vans or jeeps can be hired for longer periods of time. Hong Kongers are adept at locating these.

Auto rickshaws: Sometimes these are available for hire in places where taxis are expensive or scarce.

Bicycle rickshaws: In the flatter areas of China this is a convenient, though primitive way of getting around. In places like Qufu or Chengdu you can be pedalled all over town and confront your slavemaster feelings as you tour.

Walking: Walking in the cities and the countryside is a marvellous way to learn about a place. The biggest hazard is the blaring of horns. If you get far away from the tourist areas you might begin to feel like the Pied Piper, however, as a parade quickly develops. A small compass can help to orient you in the cities. In the dreary overcast conditions so often prevalent, it is easy to become confused in the maze of winding streets and the name of your hotel written in Chinese will be of help in getting directions home. Thus prepared, we suggest that you set out walking without fear.

Money

Take your money in the form of a well-known brand of travellers' cheques. The exchange rate for them is more favourable than for cash. All major hotels will be able to exchange your travellers' cheques and the rate is uniform throughout China. On occasions US dollars in small denominations might prove convenient.

Credit cards can be used at large hotels and the stores within them. Places that take these cards, however, are the most expensive and might do damage to your budget.

China has operated for years with two types of currency. One is called Foreign Exchange Certificates (FEC), the other Renminbi (RMB), or people's money. Foreign Exchange Certificates are the bane of a traveller's existence in China. Rumours circulate constantly that they are to be eliminated, but it hasn't happened yet.

FEC, if they still exist when you are in China, will be worth somewhat more than RMB. The rate on the black market has varied on our trips from almost equal to about two to one. The latter rate means that everybody tries to coerce you into paying them with FEC instead of RMB. FEC are exchanged for RMB on the black market, so if a taxi driver or shopkeeper cons you into paying with FEC they pocket the difference. You will almost always have to pay for your hotel, transport, and Friendship Store purchases with FEC. Local stores, private restaurants, taxis, etc should be paid for with RMB even though it is common for taxi drivers to have a sticker on their window saying 'Please pay with FEC'.

Foreign Exchange Certificates are clearly marked and their denomination is easy to understand. With Renminbi the larger notes can be distinguished easily and the smaller ones are worth so little that it doesn't matter.

The three smallest notes, which you will probably never use unless you travel on city buses, are for 1, 2 and 5 fen. A hundred fen equals one yuan in the standard decimal system progression; a yuan is worth about 20-25 pence (30-40 US cents).

The most expensive hotels will peg their rates to the US dollar, so any fluctuation in the value of the yuan will not affect their charges.

Shopping

Shopping in China used to be limited to Friendship Stores, but now there are numerous other possibilities. Many of them are mentioned in this book.

The old standbys — silk, antiques, cashmere, embroidery, down products, pottery and jade — are still available. The prices for these items are much more reasonable in the local department stores but the quality and quantity are usually inferior.

To take antiques out of China they must be stamped with an official seal and accompanied by a receipt from a government store. Better buys are often found in Hong Kong or London!

Books, maps, reproductions, posters, children's books printed in English, and rubbings come in large and interesting variety and make excellent souvenirs and gifts. Though their printing and paper is not always of good quality their prices are excellent.

Traditional objects still in daily use such as silk and paper fans, chopsticks, abacuses, scales, name seals and chops, mah jong sets, and calligraphy equipment all have functional style and grace.

Clothing tends to be ill fitting with zips and buttons that work poorly. Clothing manufactured in China for export will usually not appear on the shelves there.

Many items of furs, ivory, and feathers come from endangered species. If you purchase something in this category it may well be confiscated when you get home.

In some cities, especially Chengdu, artists sell their work on the pavements near the tourist hotels.

Language

An inevitable question about travelling in China is, 'Is language a problem?' Indeed it is!

How to Use This Book

English is spoken in the better hotels, restaurants, shopping areas that cater for tourists, and CITS offices. In smaller cities CAAC offices, at bus and train stations the 'English expert' might get out a fine 'Good morning. Can I help you?' and that's the extent of their expertise. These instances as well as daily needs call for a little preparation.

A good phrasebook is vital to survival for any independent wandering. A phrasebook will give you not only the Chinese characters as a translation of the English but also the pinyin (the romanisation of the Chinese language). The phonetics of pinyin are not easy to learn without a teacher. If you fail to be understood when you say the word (as will most likely happen) you can point to the characters. The Chinese people are always very relieved once they realise they can understand your question.

Their fear of not understanding is part of the problem. They are so sure that it is impossible that most will avoid any contact with you. Assistants in shops will frequently disappear when they spy a foreigner coming or else become extremely busy.

Chinese is not easy to pick up along the way. A fair amount of fundamentals is needed to get beyond the first few words. Of course if you are fortunate enough to have a Chinese friend to teach you a few key phrases it will be of great value. People appreciate your trying to learn their language and will show it in their dealings with you.

Phrasebooks: There are many on the market. We suggest Barron's *Chinese At A Glance* for several reasons. Most importantly it is both a phrase book and a dictionary. The dictionary is needed when you want a certain word and can't remember where in the book you might have seen it. It has an excellent selection of phrases and the layout is such that you can clearly point to a character. it is also sturdy, bound to last, and lightweight.

China Phrasebook by Lonely Planet is smaller in both size and scope. It offers a limited number of well chosen phrases.

A good dictionary available at bookshops in Hong Kong is the *Pocket English-Chinese* (pinyin) *Dictionary*. This book can be helpful if you intend to learn more than the basic phrases.

The foreign language bookshops in China are excellent places to browse and at times have English-to-Chinese dictionaries in a variety of sizes. A Chinese-to-English dictionary is of little benefit because it takes a long time to look up a word. They also carry a phrase book *Say it in Chinese* which is adequate.

The Berlitz phrase book is filled with the standard phrases, most of which are inappropriate for individuals travelling in China.

Translation problems: As we sit here hidden behind piles of books on China we are beginning to feel that a little knowledge is indeed a dangerous thing. There is a vast variety of contradicting information available.

Be it a dish or a historical monument, the first problem is to work out the name of the thing that you wish to talk about. In a country as old as China, occupied over the centuries by so many foreign countries, names undergo many changes.

Next you are faced with the question of how to write the word in Roman letters. Almost everyone has now opted for the new pinyin instead of the old Wade-Giles and Lessing system. Many, however, continue to use Peking instead of Beijing or Canton instead of Guangzhou. In this book we have decided to use only pinyin, though we do succumb to 'Peking Duck' instead of 'Beijing Duck'.

Even addresses pose a dilemma. We sometimes find one address on site and different ones in different books. Phone numbers are also a problem. Our experience has been that almost no number listed in a guidebook has been valid.

As you travel about laden down with guidebooks, maps, and information gathered from fellow travellers, we're sure you will create your own list of confusing contradictions.

Staying in touch

Mail: No matter what you may read or hear about being able to receive mail at hotels or post offices in China, it seldom works out. We probably do not get more than one out of every 20 letters sent to us when we are on the move. If you live in one place it is different. If you are going to be gone less than a month, don't even think about having mail sent to you except at the YMCA in Hong Kong.

You will have no trouble sending letters out of China. We haven't experienced any problems with the scores of letters and packages we've sent.

Telex: These have a way of going astray. The garbled notice announcing that you have a telex will be posted on some bulletin board for years, and maybe on your second or third trip to China you can pick it up.

Telephones: The better hotel rooms in China have phones which you can use to call overseas. There will be a form in the room to fill in and give to the floor attendant. The connection goes through within a few minutes. Reversed charge calls are usually easier and cheaper to make.

Our suggestion is that you choose one person at home to phone periodically. Inform others that you will be in contact with this person every so many days and that messages can be relayed through them. This keeps you from having to place more than one phone call at a time.

Sending packages: Packages can only be sent from larger post offices which have a customs agent assigned there, All packages must be examined before being sealed to prevent antiques or other prohibited merchandise being shipped out of the country.

The procedure for sending a package is to take your merchandise unsealed to the post office where it will be examined. If it is old or looks old then it will need an official wax seal on it and must be accompanied by a receipt from a government store. Then you pack it, weigh it, and fill in three sets of forms. If it is a cardboard box it must be wrapped in brown paper and sealed. An alternative is to pack the goods in a linen bag and sew it up.

Insuring the contents is nearly impossible.

This is a reasonable, dependable way of getting excess merchandise home. Allow for two to three months for a package to arrive by surface mail, or a couple of weeks by airmail.

The most convenient place in China from which to send packages is the main post office in Shanghai. Another good spot is the post office in the Jinjiang Hotel in Chengdu. Before mailing a parcel it is wise to visit the post office to find what packaging materials they have available. The two mentioned often have everything you might need. The Beijing International Post Office is better than most and can be used if necessary.

Plan on spending at least two hours to send a parcel. See the regulations from your own country for the proper procedures for identifying packages to avoid paying duty.

Information and assistance

Obtaining valid current information about travel in China is at best a piecemeal procedure. Contrary to what one might expect of a centrally controlled Communist country there is no one entity with overall responsibility. Each agency is self contained, jealous, and even secretive in its operation. From the lowest clerk on up everyone considers his position as one of absolute authority and runs it as his own fiefdom.

Inside China: China International Travel Service (CITS) is the place to begin. Within limits they can arrange hotels, transport, and sightseeing.

Hotels: CITS controls some hotels and has working relations with others where they are able to make reservations. To confuse matters, individual CITS offices have their own arrangements with different hotels. In general, each office can book rooms in CITS hotels within its own city and at times can make reservations at CITS hotels in other cities. In some places such as Beijing a CITS hotel booking can't be made at the hotel, but rather at a CITS office. CITS usually cannot make reservations in privately owned or joint venture hotels,. These you can do directly or through a travel agent.

Transport: The local CITS offices can usually arrange the purchase of tickets to your next destination, though they cannot arrange tickets from a second to a third destination. They require several days advance notice, because in order to buy a ticket someone from that office must queue just like everyone else. In fact it can be more difficult for them because at times limits are put on the number of tickets they are allowed to purchase.

The central CITS office in Beijing (see the address in the back of this book) can work with your local travel agent in making arrangements for individual travel in China. These arrangements have to be made with prior payment, a minimum of a month in advance, and no cancellations or schedule changes are allowed. These tickets and vouchers are not always dependable, however, since they are subject to the whims of local technocrats.

Local sightseeing: CITS can arrange at considerable expense a private car with driver and English speaking guide for your local excursions. They offer group tours at reasonable prices if enough people sign up.

Private travel agents: The government's encouragement of private enterprise is proving to be a boon for the individual traveller. Non-government travel agents are appearing in shops. Sometimes they reserve blocks of rooms for tour groups and have these rooms available for individual travellers when unoccupied. They also offer local sightseeing tours and occasionally some long distance bus services. For example, in Tibet they are hiring landrovers by the day and have set up a minibus service from Lhasa to Golmud in direct competition with the government buses. Even some CITS employees moonlight as private agents and numerous unaffiliated individuals hang around tourist-frequented restaurants offering to help make travel arrangements.

Provincial governments are also competing for the tourist money by developing regional airlines, hotels and related services. Since their objective is to attract the tourist, their quality is usually superior to that of the frequently inadequate facilities offered by the central government. Often the CITS employees have no knowledge of these services.

Receptionists: As a service to their guest, the receptionists of some hotels are offering some of the same assistance as CITS. This is especially true in the smaller, more remote areas. One of the fascinations of travelling in China is watching private enterprise develop to meet expanding needs.

Local Chinese people: The Chinese, who are just beginning to travel themselves, are a potential source of information. Most of them are on trips organised by their work units (dan wei) and

How to Use This Book

know little about travel arrangements or how to find their way about on their own in a new area. Millions of higher level officials in both government and the military have been retired early since the mid-eighties and now have the opportunity to visit the same tourist attractions we go to China to see. A third group of Chinese are students and teachers sent by their schools on outings or to attend workshops in resort areas, especially during the summer holidays. There are even a few individual Chinese who are off travelling on their own with a backpack.

All have in common the enjoyment of their new freedom to travel, and part of the fun is the camaraderie with foreign travellers. If they speak any English at all they will make an effort to befriend you, share experiences, and if possible be of assistance. We have learned that in most cases it is better to avoid their generous offers of help. They mean well but know so little about being in unknown territory that they tend to get us into situations that we would avoid on our own.

Foreign travellers have to abide by a different set of rules. Until recently westerners ate, slept and travelled separately from the local Chinese. This division is disappearing, but it is still something to keep in mind.

Foreigners often have to buy their tickets at special booths and pay two to five times as much for the same services. To pay Chinese prices for tickets, many individual travellers have got Chinese to buy their tickets for them, sometimes sharing the price difference. Not all Chinese know that foreigners pay more, and some complications may arise when they try to get tickets for you in an effort just to be helpful.

English Corner: Most cities have an English Corner where Chinese meet to speak and practise English with each other. They hope that a native English speaker will show up and will make you most welcome. This is an excellent place to meet people who are well informed and who wish to discuss various topics in English. Their information will not necessarily help you as a tourist but you will learn more about China through these intelligent, hard-working, often self-taught people than in any other way. Any English speaker on the staff of your hotel can tell you where and when the English Corner meets. It is usually in the evening in a public park.

Other foreigners: These are your best sources of information. Businessmen, foreign experts, teachers, and students living in China know one set of information. Other fellow travellers, particularly long-term backpackers, often know another. Depending on what we want to know we'll head for the better restaurants or hotel lobbies to meet business people, the universities to meet teachers and students, or the hotel dormitories to find the backpackers.

Hong Kongers: You will learn to recognise them easily. They are in their late teens or twenties, dressed in practical sports clothes, usually in groups of four or more adorned with the latest in electronic gadgetry. China is the first country in which they can afford to travel, so they, like their mainland cousins, are having a wonderful time. They are able to get about China easily, often speak good English, and will go out of their way to help.

Many of these groups have been to China several times and now seek more remote destinations. Travelling in a self-contained group as they do, they are able to arrange vehicles to take them to out-of-the-way places. They might help you do the same or let you tag along with them.

Changes

China is changing rapidly. We can't emphasise this often enough. With each new trip we see drastic changes and sometimes they seem to happen between the time we go to bed and the time we get up. So it is with caution that we offer our information and observations, knowing that even if you use this book hot off the press much will have changed.

We foresee fees getting higher until China prices itself out of the tour group market. Then they will begin to level off. The Chinese officials who set policy have not travelled the world and do not know what they are competing against. They only know that tourists keep pounding on the door to get in, so they sometimes believe there is no limit to how high prices can go.

Services are improving as a result of tourist complaints. In hotels, shops, and restaurants the service is progressively better. Ticket offices, however, are getting worse because of the extra strain that comes with the increased volume of travel.

Private enterprise is making inroads into the tourist business. Entrepreneurs are offering bus services for both local tours and long distances, even regional airlines are developing. Privately owned restaurants, food stands, and markets are appearing all over. Most private businesses offer better service than the government versions.

As a traveller the biggest difference is that you are no longer isolated from the Chinese. The Chinese standard of living is improving and they are now on the road. You will now find them sharing soft sleeper with you on the trains, staying in rooms next to yours in hotels and eating in all the better restaurants.

Once upon a time you'd walk out of the Friendship Stores and find groups of locals peering through the partially opened door. Now they are in there shopping too. The next development is already apparent: the Friendship Stores are no longer necessary. The smart traveller goes to the local shops where the prices are

How to Use This Book

better, the service more pleasant, and the merchandise approximately the same if not more varied.

You may wonder why with all these rapid changes we often mention personnel in particular positions, as if we expect them to be still there. That is because we do. As of now, it is almost impossible for a person to change his or her job in China.

Recommended reading

China: A Travel Survival Kit by Alan Samagalski and Michael Buckley, Lonely Planet Publications, Victoria, Australia 1987 (available from most good bookshops), is an invaluable book for the traveller moving about on his own — the budget travellers' Bible. Some of the author's frustration in gathering information shows through in unnecessarily negative comments. Nevertheless, it would be hard to imagine getting off the beaten track without this book.

Fielding's People's Republic of China by Ruth Lor Malloy and Priscilla Liang Hsu, William Morrow & Company, New York, 1987, is more suitable for someone on an escorted tour or less concerned with expenses. It contains a great deal of valuable information but doesn't have the practical details that let you strike off on your own. Because of the authors' Chinese heritage they help the reader avoid misunderstandings arising from cultural differences. Read it even if you don't take it with you.

Other guidebooks: *Nagel's Encyclopedia-Guide China*, Nagel Publishers, Geneva, Paris, Munich, 1984. *The China Guidebook* by Fredric Kaplan, Julian Sobin, Arne deKeijzer, Houghton Mifflin Company, Boston; Eurasia Press, New York, 1987. *China On Your Own* by Russell and Penny Jennings and Michael R. Kelsey, Cordee Ltd, 1985. *Tibet: A Travel Survival Kit* by Michael Buckley and Robert Strauss, Lonely Planet Publications, 1986. *China Companion* by Evelyne Garside, André Deutsch, London, 1982.

Books to read before you go: Of many books written about China we have found particularly helpful for our travels the following: *CHINA Alive in the Bitter Sea* by Fox Butterfield, Coronet, London 1983. *The Chinese* by David Bonavia, Lippincott & Cromwell, New York 1980. *The Chinese, Portrait of a People* by John Fraser, 1980, Summit Books, New York. *Red Star over China* by Edgar Snow, Penquin Books, London. Han Suyin — any and all of her books.

Contemporary fiction by Chinese writers is available in English translation at bookshops in China. The following are generally well written and give insight into Chinese thinking: *A Small Town Called Hibiscus* by GuHua. *All The Colours of the Rainbow* by Jiang Zilong. *The Diary of a Young English Teacher* by Sam Ginsbourg. *Catkin Willow Flats* by Liu Shaotang. *Contemporary Chinese Short Stories*. *Seven Contemporary Chinese Women Writers*.

MEI YOU
GETTING WHAT YOU WANT

Unfortunately, one of the first expressions you will learn as an independent traveller in China is 'Mei you' (pronounced 'may-o' and translated literally as 'Not have'). A traveller comes to understand it as, 'For some reason that you'll never understand, so I'm not even going to try to explain it to you, I'm not going to give you what you want'.

You will be told 'Mei you' meaning there are no rooms, only to see the next person in line get one without question. The same will hold true for train or plane tickets, being served dinner at a late hour, or just about anything you want to do.

Our first time in China we were the ones to receive the 'Mei you' treatment. By the third time we joined the ranks of 'For you...of course'.

Never lose your composure or cause your Chinese host to lose face, but **never take 'mei you' for an answer.**

They say, 'Mei you'. You smile and don't budge an inch. If at a counter or desk, stay there. Being at the counter is your advantage point. They still have to do something about you. If they get you to leave, they have won. Keep smiling and asking the same question until you decide to switch strategies. The next step is to reinforce your attack by offering alternatives. 'If we can't have a double room, can we have a room with three beds?' Is there a room without a television? A room without an air conditioner? A room with the bath down the hall? A room for just one day?

Be inventive. They will not volunteer anything. It is up to you to guess what they have!

If you still haven't achieved your goal, reach deeper into your bag of tricks. 'Ke Yi' (pronounced 'kuh ye') translates as 'can'. In Chinese personal pronouns are often omitted, so 'Ke Yi' can be used in two ways. With a positive, cheerful, affirmative tone you are conveying, 'Come on, we know you are important, intelligent, or capable enough to do this for us'. Don't forget the smile. With a questioning intonation, coupled with a puzzled (or cute if it suits your personality) look, you are asking, 'Can I?' or 'May I?' as the case may require. You are showing respect for their authority but once again forcing them to make a decision rather than just the knee-jerk response 'Mei you'.

It is conceivable that what you want is truly not available, but just hang in there until you are sure. Patience, persistence and politeness are your most powerful aids to travel in China.

ITINERARY

TOUR 1 Arrive in Hong Kong. If you pre-arranged your Chinese visa and boat passage to Xiamen, you may take the boat today instead of tomorrow. Otherwise, spend a day (or longer) exploring Hong Kong.

TOUR 2 Board the 11:30 am boat for the overnight trip to Xiamen.

TOUR 3 This morning you'll wake up in China. In the afternoon, see the sights of Xiamen: Nanputu Temple, Xiamen University and Gulangi Island.

TOUR 4 Take a 2-hour taxi ride through the countryside to the small town of Quanzhou. See the lovely temple and a museum housing the remains of an ocean-going junk. Return to Xiamen. (**OPTION:** Catch the overnight train to the Chinese resort of Wuyi Shan, where you can stay in a mountaintop monastery.)

TOUR 5 Take the train to Hangzhou. Stroll around West Lake, one of China's most popular tourist spots. Most of the Chinese people you'll meet there are also on holiday, so you'll find them unusually open and friendly. (**OPTION:** By rearranging the next week of this itinerary you can visit the island sacred mountain Putuo Shan, rarely visited by westerners.)

TOUR 6 Travel by train to Shaoxing, a charming small town with narrow lanes, twisting canals, craftsmen and villagers — and almost no tourists. Visit 6th century Emperor Yu Mausoleum.

TOUR 7 Return to Hangzhou in either the morning or the afternoon.

TOUR 8 Take an early morning train to Shanghai, arriving at about noon. Stroll through Huangpu Park and the Bund, and end your day with a drink at the Jazz Club in the Peace Hotel.

TOUR 9 Wander the streets of Shanghai, China's most European-feeling city. Browse through bookshops and calligraphy shops on your way to the Shanghai Museum.

TOUR 10 Discover Shanghai's colonial era French Section. Stop at shops selling arts, crafts and antiques on your way to Yuyuan Gardens.

Itinerary

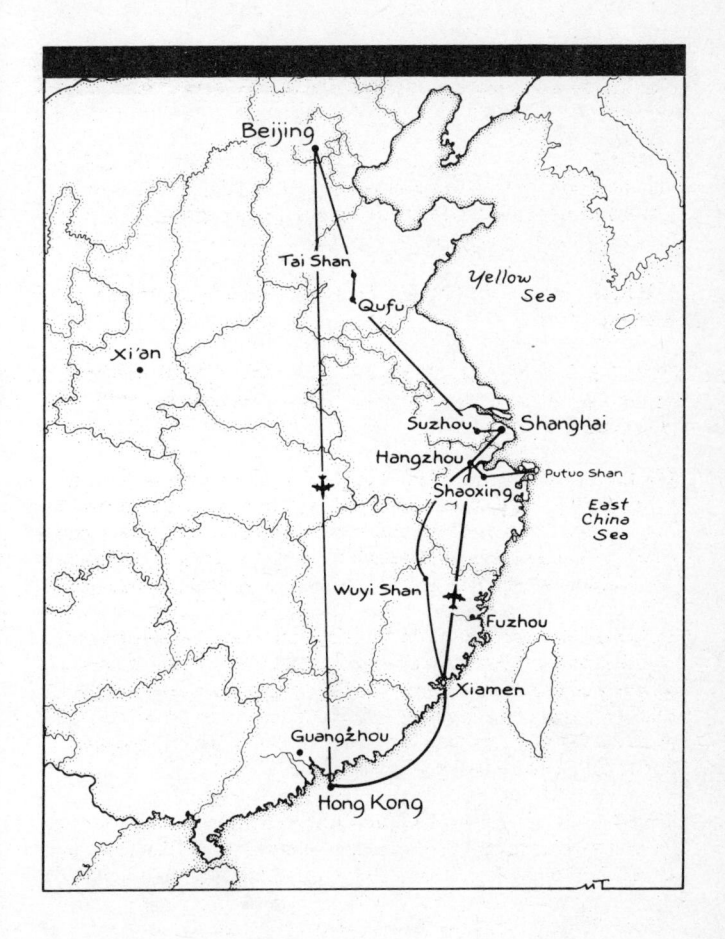

TOUR 11 Take a day trip to the town of Suzhou to see the world's best gardens, models for the famous Zen gardens of Japan. Relax at the teahouse in the Master of the Nets Garden, a portion of which is reproduced in New York's Metropolitan Museum of Art.

TOUR 12 Train and bus will take you to Qufu, birthplace of the great Chinese philosopher Confucius. Visit the Confucian Temple, wander in the Confucian Forest, and stay the night at Confucian Mansions. The Mansions were the home of Confucius' descendants for 14 centuries, up to the revolution; now it is a hotel.

TOUR 13 Travel by bus to Tai Shan, the most revered and popular of China's sacred mountains and the subject of paintings and poetry for many centuries. Stay at your choice of hotels at the foot of the mountain, midway, or on the summit for an incomparable sunrise view.

TOUR 14 Leave Tai Shan in the morning for an all-day train journey and an early evening arrival in Beijing.

TOUR 15 Spend your first day in Beijing touring the central city. Highlights will include Tianamen Square, the Forbidden City and arts and crafts shopping. See a Chinese opera tonight.

TOUR 16 Take an all-day tour to the most famous sight in China, the Great Wall. On the way you'll visit the Ming Tombs. Upon returning to the city, enjoy a Peking duck dinner.

TOUR 17 This is a day of relaxed sightseeing, wandering and shopping. Start at the Palace of Eternal Harmony, then visit the Confucius Temple, North Sea Park and the Nationalities Cultural Palace. Along the way you'll be tempted by dozens of shops selling arts, crafts, food and fine, reasonably priced silk products.

TOUR 18 An all-day sightseeing tour will take you to Fragrant Hills park, the Temple of the Sleeping Buddha, the Temple of Awareness and the Summer Palace.

TOUR 19 Spend your final day in China wandering Beijing on your own, perhaps doing last-minute shopping at stores you discovered earlier. (This is a 'slack' day for itinerary flexibility. You can omit it if you elected to take one of the 'Options' to the sacred mountains Wuyi Shan and Putuo Shan described earlier, or to spend an extra day at one of your earlier destinations.)

TOUR 20 Fly from Beijing to Hong Kong.

TOUR 21 Free rest day in Hong Kong.

TOUR 22 Fly home from Hong Kong.

TOUR 1
HONG KONG

Today you arrive in Hong Kong. If you arranged your boat ticket to Xiamen and your Chinese visa before you left home, you may elect to take the boat today instead of tomorrow and recover from jet lag during the cruise. If so, turn to 'Tour 2'. The following information is for those who wish to spend the day (or longer) sampling the temptations of Hong Kong.

Suggested Schedule	
6:00	Breakfast on plane.
9:00	Arrive at Hong Kong Airport
11.:00	Go to the pier and board the boat for the overnight trip to Xiamen; OR check into your Hong Kong hotel and spend a leisurely afternoon shopping and eating.
	Jet lag will decide your bedtime.

Arrival
Hong Kong airport is conveniently located, signs are in English and it is easy to find your way around. Pick up your luggage, clear entry formalities, and head for the money exchange counter.

Change only £5-£10 or US $10-$20 — the rate in town will be much better. Make sure you get five Hong Kong dollars in coins per person for the bus fare into town, exact fare is required. Numerous free maps of Hong Kong are available at the airport, as well as at hotels and tourist shops. Exit at the end of the building and get onto bus number A1, which stops at numerous hotels, including the YMCA, on its run to the Star Ferry. Recorded announcements will tell you what bus stops are coming up and which stop is for which hotel. Get off across the street from the YMCA where you have long ago made reservations....

Hotels
Our Hong Kong hotel recommendation begins and ends with the **YMCA** on Salisbury Road in Kowloon. It has an excellent location, good variety of rooms and prices, friendly staff, bookshop, library, machine for instant visa photos and, most important, other travellers from whom you can extract information. To meet these travellers we often breakfast there. Double rooms are in the £15-£25 (US$25-$40) price range. With

Hong Kong

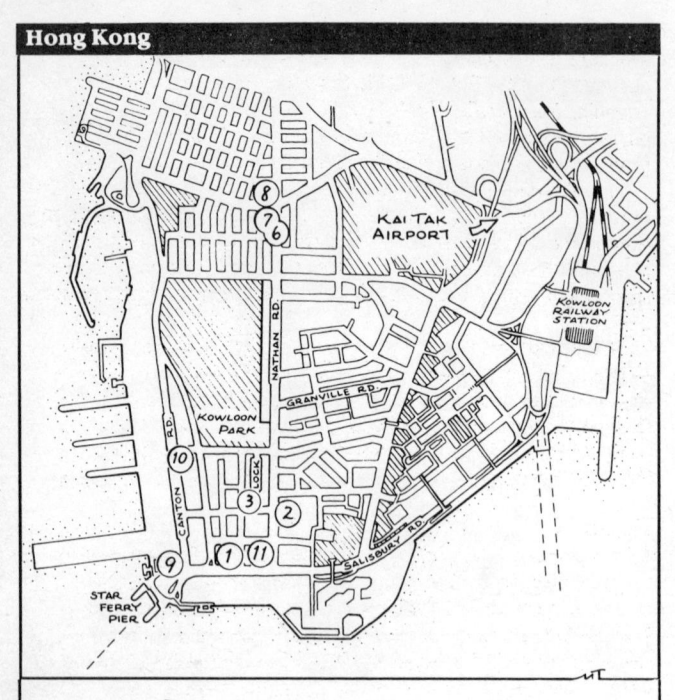

1. YMCA
2. Chung King Mansions
3. Swindon Books
4. New Delhi Restaurant
5. Shamrock Restaurant
6. Jewelry Store/Money Exchange
7. C.A.C.
8. Yue Hwa Chinese Products
9. Star Ferry Building
10. Silvercord Building
11. Peninsula Hotel

the opening of a new addition in 1986, many more rooms are available to alleviate the chronic shortage. Reservations are needed. P.O. Box 95096 T.S.T. Kowloon, Hong Kong. Cable: Triangle, Telex 31274 HYMCA HX, telephone 3-692211. One day's payment in advance is required to confirm booking, and reservations are not ordinarily taken over the phone.

The alternative choices go either up or down from here. At the bottom, many people stay in a building called the **Chung-King Mansions**, which bear no resemblance to the name. This high-rise building is straight out of Calcutta and is destined to burn some night taking hundreds of lives. The lifts are a pickpocket's delight.

At the upper end of the price range, every major hotel chain — Hyatt, Sheraton, Hilton, etc — is represented in Hong Kong. Take your pick. For a splash amid Old World elegance, the **Peninsula**, at the corner of Salisbury Road and Nathan Road (telex 4382) would be great fun, though expensive at £100 (US$175) for standard accommodation, £105 (US$185) for deluxe.

Food

'Dim sum' is a lunch made up of many small dishes which come to your table on trolleys. You pick what you want and keep choosing more dishes through the course of the meal. The waitress will stamp your card each time you take a dish, or else calculate your bill from the number of empty plates on your table. It adds up to a very pleasant way of dining.

If you enjoy Indian cooking, the **New Delhi Restaurant** at 53 Cameron Road is excellent. We've feasted there on £6 ($10) for two. One of the most gracious ways to recuperate from a hard day in Hong Kong is afternoon tea in the lobby of the Peninsula Hotel. Most major hotels serve vast western-style buffets, which you might particularly enjoy when you return to Hong Kong at the end of your China tour.

See the suggested walks, below, for additional eating options.

Shopping

One of the world's most exciting cities, Hong Kong has evolved from being a port for sailors and cheap merchandise into one of the world's premier banking centres. Its essence is money. Hong Kongers love their little place and rush about fulfilling their civic duty, that is, to spend and make money. It is easy to get caught up in a buying frenzy.

The Hong Kong of 15 to 20 years ago is no more. The streets full of tailors making inexpensive clothing, bargains on cameras, etc are still there, but finding them during a short visit will take some effort. Many things will be cheaper and of guaranteed quality in the discount stores at home.

To find these shopping bargains begin in the bookshops. Browse through the several books available on shopping in Hong Kong, and perhaps buy one. Bookshops in general are the best place to gather information about Asia. Arriving in Hong Kong straight from your home country, book-browsing aids the mental transition to the Orient. The YMCA has an excellent bookshop and a lending library. A few blocks away, on Lock Road, behind the Hyatt, is Swindon Books, which is the best in town. This is the time to buy your Chinese railway timetable in English, your phrasebook and/or dictionary, and a map of China both in pinyin and Chinese characters.

Somewhere in Hong Kong every possible type of merchandise can be found. Among the more popular items for travellers are: clothing, jewellery, glasses, cameras, radios and all high tech products.

Stay with reputable shops for electronic merchandise. As a rule, the places offering the cheapest prices are selling faulty equipment that will not live up to your expectations. Inspection stickers and warranties are not dependable.

We always take time to explore the various shopping arcades known as China Arts and Crafts or CAC. These shops carry merchandise from China. Look around carefully, but don't buy anything until you come back from China. You might get it cheaper there.

Suggested shopping and eating walk 1

There are some major CAC buildings within easy walking distance of the YMCA. Our favourite one is about a twenty minute walk up Nathan Road (see map). We always make an expedition of it by stopping in the great variety of shops along the way. Granville Road, with its abundance of bargain clothing shops, is six blocks up Nathan Road. On Granville Road near the corner, is another well-stocked bookshop.

Back to Nathan Road and continuing on down on the right is a dim sum restaurant with a gaudy golden door leading upstairs. This is a friendly and popular place, but sometimes the food is too greasy. Just a little way on is a small cafe and bakery. The Shamrock restaurant is across the street and down about a block, it also has a good dim sum lunch. Near the Shamrock is a large jewellery store with three money exchange windows inside on the left. They consistently give the best exchange rate. (Many other places promise one rate on their signs but, in fact, offer another.)

Past the Shamrock is the CAC and on a corner half a block further down is the YueHwa Chinese products store which carries a less touristy line of Chinese products. Investigate the supermarket in the basement. Their kitchen supply and hardware section contains things you will rarely find in China.

Suggested shopping and eating walk 2
(shorter)
Going the other direction from the YMCA is the Star Ferry. The large building to the right before the ferry is known as the Star Ferry Building (logical). It contains a CAC store and also a Hong Kong Student Travel office on the 17th floor.

Around the corner from here and down Canton Road a couple of blocks is the Silvercord Building, another Chinese government building selling Chinese products. It also has a dim sum restaurant on the 3rd floor, where they will try to force you into a very dull, formal, and expensive room; insist on sitting with the masses. Just do like the locals and continue in until you find empty seats.

Items to buy in Hong Kong
There are four items you'll need to pick up before leaving Hong Kong. One is a current CAAC timetable, which you can easily get from a travel agency in Hong Kong but not readily in China. The other three are available from a bookshop though you might have to shop around: A China Railway Timetable in English will be invaluable if you do any train travel. You'll need a map of China with large print written in both pinyin and Chinese characters so you can point to the Chinese characters when you can't make your attempts to pronounce place-names understood. The final item you'll want is a phrase book. See the language section of **How To Use This Book** for suggestions.

On a short trip of three or four weeks don't expect to be able to find everyday necessities. They are available, and you will come across them from time to time, but shopping in China is like the Zen experience of enlightenment — if you search for it you cannot find it. Take things with you instead of planning to pick them up along the way.

TOUR 2
HONG KONG – XIAMEN

Board the boat from Hong Kong to Xiamen at 11:00 am. After an overnight trip, you'll be in China first thing the next morning.

Suggested Schedule

Morning	Free in Hong Kong until mid-morning.
10:30	Taxi to the Tai-Kok-Tsui Ferry Pier.
11:00	Board ship for overnight trip to Xiamen. Lunch on board.

Transport: Hong Kong to Xiamen (overnight)

A taxi to the terminal will cost HK $12 to $15 (about £1.20 or US $2). The exit procedures are fairly straightforward. Stand in one queue after another until you reach the shuttle ferry for the trip out to the big boat anchored in the harbour.

The boat to Xiamen is operated by Fujian Province Shipping Corporation, China. The Hong Kong general agent is Yick Fung Shipping & Enterprises Co, Ltd. **To buy your tickets in advance**, ask your local travel agent or write to any of the Hong Kong travel agencies mentioned in this book. A first-class cabin with private bath costs about £60 (US$100) for two people. Second class without a private bath costs only a few pounds less. Dormitories come in various sizes and prices.

As you board the ship (an old European one) you'll be directed to your cabin. Be forewarned, this is not the QE II. Your cabin will have two bunks, one above the other. First-class cabins have private baths, otherwise second class has basins in the rooms and a bath across the hall. Wander around and locate the dining rooms, marked '1' and '2'. As the boat gets underway, lunch will be served in No. 1 dining room. Nothing fancy — passengers help themselves to the steamed rice from a central kettle. If you desire a beer with your meal, give the waiter the price in Hong Kong dollars and he'll bring it from the bar.

Most of your fellow passengers are expatriate Chinese returning to their homeland, often to visit relatives in Fujian Province or elsewhere in China. Some of the passengers are returning to China for the first time in fifty years. Children, on their way to see grandma and grandpa for the first time, act as if it were Christmas Eve. An air of excitement fills the ship. Though they come from all parts of the world, many passengers speak

English. You can learn a great deal by conversing with them.

After eating, find a spot on the deck to watch as the ship makes its way through Hong Kong Harbour and out to the South China Sea. As the ship heads north, it will pass colourful Chinese junks that work the offshore fishing grounds.

If you have connected directly to this ship from your flight to Hong Kong, it's time for a shower and a nap. Otherwise there is a reading room on board with Chinese magazines and usually a few recent copies of the English language newspaper *The China Daily*. Browse and get an idea of what has been happening in China, glancing out of the window occasionally for a glimpse of the red sails in the sunset.

If the boat is full enough to require two dinner servings, coupons will be brought to your room. Foreigners are usually given the first sitting.

Go to bed early, sleep all night, and wake up in China.

TOUR 3
XIAMEN

This is the day you've been waiting for. You will awake in China. After arranging your onward travel tickets at the CITS office (which hopefully will not take too long), enjoy a pleasant day of lazy strolling, a visit to a temple, and good eating.

Suggested Schedule

Arrive in Xiamen.
Check into your hotel.
Make onward travel arrangements.
Lunch at hotel (or at Nanputu Temple).
Visit Nanputu Temple and the University.
Gulangu Island or Celestial Yacht Builders.
Sunset cocktails at your hotel, dinner.

Arriving in China

You'll awake as the ship is approaching Xiamen. There will be a thermos of hot water and some packets of tea in the room. Furnish your own instant coffee. The frenzy aboard the boat will make you think there are only a few seconds to prepare for departure. Actually you probably have a couple of hours.

The dining room serves a Chinese breakfast of rice gruel called kongee which most westerners never learn to like, but be sociable and at least take a look. You will be able to get a good western-style breakfast at the Lujiang Hotel in Xiamen.

As you stand on deck, Xiamen is to the right of where the ship ties up. The small island on your left with the red domed building dominating the view is called Gulangu. On the Xiamen side, a long hill leads to the south where you can see the Temple of Nanputu and the adjoining Xiamen University on the hillside.

Chinese entry formalities are divided between ship and shore. Fill out the forms which are passed out, clear the aboardship portion in No. 1 dining room, and receive a medallion that will be collected as you go ashore. The first building on the left is for claiming extra baggage. Skip it and go ahead to the building where you clear customs. Entry is very simple. Change £5-£10 (US$10-$20) at the money counter, and walk out of the building and up the ramp to where people are waiting to greet disembarking passengers.

Taxis and rickshaws will be available there.

Lodging

From where the ship ties up alongside the pier, the **Lujiang Hotel** is a couple of hundred yards to the north — to your left against a one-way road, less than a 10-minute walk along the waterfront. Either walk or take some conveyance to the hotel. Due to the numerous one-way streets, a taxi will have to travel about a mile to get there. When checking in, insist on an upper-storey room facing the water. The coffee shop serves a good breakfast. Quality in this hotel seems to depend on the floor. We have had excellent rooms here; other people we know haven't. If you don't get a room you like, change to another floor. Prices are in the £12 ($20) range for a double.

Eight hotels in Xiamen accept foreigners (you); the Lujiang is the most convenient. Other good places to stay include the **Seaview Garden Tourist Village** on Gulangu Island, with doubles from £10-£15 ($15-$25). It has a rural peaceful setting on lovely grounds near the sea. There are eight different buildings with quality ranging from very poor to very good. Mosquitos and dampness are factors to keep in mind as you examine rooms. No cars are allowed on this island, a blessing in China as you'll soon learn. The disadvantage in staying here for a visit of just a day or two to Xiamen is the inconvenience of taking ferries.

The **Xiamen Mandarin Hotel** is quite lovely, but expensive. The **Overseas Chinese Hotel** is in a large, unappealing structure with plain though adequate rooms costing £10-£20 ($15-$30) for a double. Consider these as back-ups in case nothing else is available.

Property is being developed all along the coast of Fujian Province, and several additional hotels are planned.

Food

The food is good almost anywhere in Xiamen. The main restaurant in the Lujiang Hotel has excellent local specialities, particularly fish and seafood dishes. For western food, the resident foreigners head for the Overseas Chinese Hotel. Street eating in the small open restaurants will spoil you for the rest of China. The assortment of seafood on the streets near the Lujiang and Overseas Chinese Hotels creates an embarrassment of riches. It's all so appetising you'll have a hard time deciding where and what to eat.

At sunset the rooftop bar at the Lujiang Hotel is a lovely spot to have a drink before setting off to find a small nearby restaurant for dinner. This is one of the few places in China where you can find a place to eat after sunset.

Xiamen

厦门

1. 鹭江宾馆   Lujiang Hotel
   鼓浪屿   Gulangyu Island
2. 观海旅游村   Seaview Garden
3. 北京饭店   Mandarin Hotel
4. 南普陀   Overseas Chinese Hotel
5. 华侨旅馆   Nanputu Temple

Transport arrangements

The first thing to do upon arrival in any Chinese city is to arrange onward transportation. There are several ways to go north from Xiamen depending on which options you choose in your itinerary. The main itinerary outlined in this book puts you on an early afternoon twice-weekly flight to Hangzhou. The cost is less than £30 ($50).

Tour 3

An option involving some hard travel is to take the train inland to Wuyi Shan. This is one of our favourite places in China, and can be one of your most memorable experiences too — but only if you're prepared to rough it. Take an overnight soft sleeper from Xiamen to Nanping, and connect by bus on to Wuyi Shan. (See Wuyi Shan Option in 'Tour 4' for details.)

A second option takes you directly into Shanghai on one of the daily 1½-hour flights, allowing you to loop back and visit the island of Putuo Shan, then to Ningbo, Shaoxing, Hangzhou and back to Shanghai. (See Putuo Shan option in 'Tour 5' for details.) The cost is about £30 ($50). Departure times vary depending on the day of the week.

Xiamen is developing as a major international tourist destination. Flights into and out of the city are becoming more frequent, so flight schedules and fares may change at any time.

To make any of these arrangements, see the helpful CITS people at the Lujiang or Overseas Chinese Hotel, or ask the receptionists.

Getting around

Ferries to Gulangu Island leave directly across the street from the Lujiang Hotel.

Xiamen's three bus routes look like a three-pointed star crossing in the centre of town. Two have their terminals at the ferry: Bus No. 3 runs from the ferry to the train station, while Bus No. 2 goes to the University area and Nanputu Temple. Bus No. 1 connects the university and the train station. To get to both Nanputu Temple and the University, take Bus No. 2 to the end of the line.

Sightseeing highlights

● ● ● **Nanputu Temple:** This Buddhist temple was built over a thousand years ago during the Tang dynasty. Destroyed during a battle in the Ming dynasty, it was rebuilt in the Qing. The temple is in good condition and makes for a lovely, serene introduction to classic temple design. Be sure to climb the cliffs behind the temple. 'Buddha' written in giant red characters cut into the rock will widen your eyes, as will the view of the city.

● **Xiamen University** was built with funds from overseas Chinese. Though the architecture is basic 20th-century brick and cement block, it does have a certain presence and is your best opportunity to see a pleasant Chinese campus. There is a museum, too, but neither of us can think of anything positive to say about it.

● ● ● **Gulangu Island** affords some interesting street wandering. Make a point of visiting the Seaview Gardens Tourist Hotel if you are nearby. Otherwise, head for high ground. From there, choose a destination. Then strike off towards it. The beaches and swimming are so-so. Two ferries make the five-minute trip to this island, one to the Seaview Hotel and the other to the public pier across from the Lujiang Hotel. Plan to go on one and return on the other.

• **Celestial Yacht Builders:** If you dream of one day buying a 48-foot fibreglass and teak cruising yacht for a fraction of its price at home, this is where they're made. Manager Malon Jackson, an old China hand, originally went to Hong Kong as a Morman missionary and has spent most of the last 20 years in Taiwan and China. Though he and the other Americans working there are busy, they're quite friendly. Time permitting, someone will show you around. Ask the receptionist at your hotel to phone and arrange a visit. The Celestial Yacht Builders is on the waterfront about halfway between the university and the Lujiang Hotel.

TOUR 4
QUANZHOU

After a good breakfast at your hotel, take a 2-hour taxi journey through the countryside to a small town where you will probably be the only 'external country person' visiting the lovely temple, interesting small museum and serene streets.

Suggested Schedule

Up early for a bird's eye view of the city coming to life.
Breakfast in the hotel.
Day trip to Quanzhou by bus or taxi.
OPTION: Depart for Wuyi Shan on the night train.

Day trip: Quanzhou

Few tourists go to Quanzhou, the next town to the north of Xiamen. The journey through the countryside is lovely. If you go by taxi, the driver will show you the Quanzhou sights, stop for lunch at the Overseas Chinese Hotel and, if you wish, also visit Jimei School Village north of Xiamen, for which China solicits donations from overseas Chinese.

Most historians agree that Quanzhou is the site where the ancient port of Zaiton once flourished. Until the 14th century, Zaiton shipped Chinese goods (satin, spices and sugar) to India, Arabia and western Asia. None of this past glory is visible, but it is a quiet, untouristed, prosperous town with narrow streets to wander as well as the handsome **Kaiyuan Temple** with its two beautiful pagodas. Though the temple was founded in the 7th century during the Tang Dynasty, the buildings standing today are from the 13th or 14th century.

Adjoining the temple is the **Museum of Overseas Communications**, housing the remains of a huge ocean-going junk excavated from nearby mudflats.

Transport

Try to locate a CITS tour going up or someone to share a taxi. Public buses don't connect readily for a one-day jaunt. A taxi will be in the £23 ($40) price range for the day.

ITINERARY OPTION: Wuyi Shan

The sacred mountain Wuyi Shan, one our favourite places in China, is easy to work into the itinerary and will add a whole new dimension to your tour. We've included Wuyi Shan and the sacred mountain Putuo Shan (see 'Tour 5) as 'Options' because each involves transportation or lodging hardships that some readers of this book may wish to bypass. If you're still recovering from jet lag, the overnight train trip and rustic monastery accommodation at Wuyi Shan may be exhausting. If you're up to the challenge, you'll remember Wuyi Shan as one of the best parts of your trip.

If you love quiet walks through mysterious trails that lead past walls, gates and doorways that tell wonderful stories in a language you don't understand, if you want to think or meditate or write poetry, and if discomfort does not ruin your day, then Wuyi Shan is for you.

Wuyi Shan Option Itinerary

DAY 4	Evening: Board the overnight train from Xiamen to Nanping.
DAY 5	Morning: Arrive in Nanping. Bus to Wuyi Shan. Overnight in Wuyi Shan
DAY 6	Explore Wuyi Shan. Stay another night.
DAY 7	Early bus to Shangrao, train to Hangzhou, overnight Hangzhou. Rejoin the main itinerary in Hangzhou on 'Tour 8' (skipping Shaoxing) or on 'Tour 6' (skipping nothing, adding two days to your trip) See 'Tour 5' for lodging, sightseeing and onward transportation details on Hangzhou.

Transport: The train for Wuyi Shan leaves at 21:58 (be sure to check the latest timetable for changes). Working backwards, you will need to arrive at the station by 21:00, so take a bus or taxi to the station by 20:30. A soft sleeper is preferable for the long journey. The train stops frequently all night, so you may want to bring something to help you sleep.

When the train arrives in Nanping at 10:17 a connecting bus to Wuyi Shan will be waiting. Make sure that some fellow passengers from the train know where you are headed so they can point you towards the right bus.

Around lunch time the bus stops for thirty minutes. You will be glad you brought your own set of chopsticks. Around 14:00 the bus stops, everyone clambers off and someone will motion to you to get off too. Look around and mutter that this sure doesn't look like what you expected.

Tour 4   55

Wuyi Shan

武夷山

上饶 Shangrao

WUYI MOUNTAIN VILLA 武夷山村

Famous Mushrooms 香菇

Swimming

Boat Ticket Booth

basketball court

JIU QU HOTEL 九曲饭店

Shops

Raft Trip

take-out point

TOWN

Bus Stop

GATE

Nanping 南平

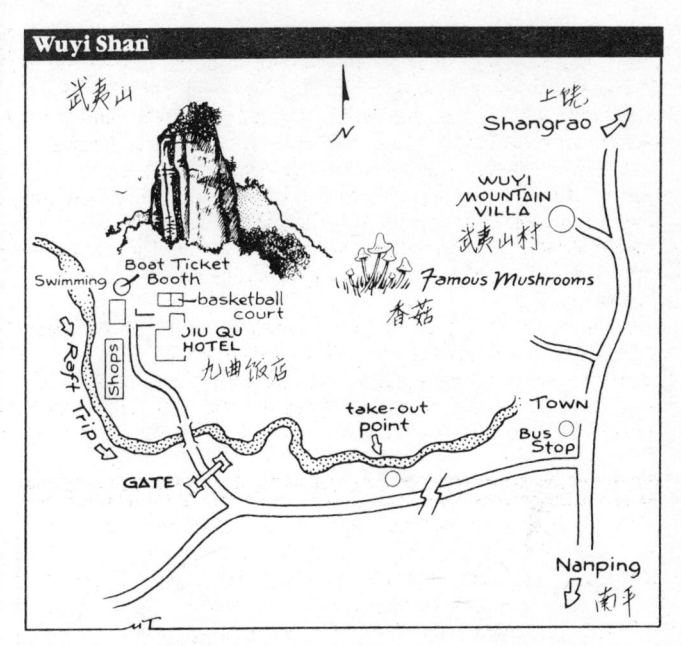

Before setting out for your hotel, cross the street and find the bus station, look for a sign outside a window. Find out when buses leave for Shangrao — usually at 6:00, 13:30 and 15:40.

Lodging: The major upper class tourist hotel, **Wuyi Mountain Villa**, is straight through town and up a side road to the left, a total of about a quarter of a mile. Though the hotel is lovely and comfortable, we have a more unusual suggestion.

Getting there is part of the adventure. A motorised tractor/pickup hybrid will be waiting to take you as far as **Jiu qu Hotel (Nine Bends Resort Hotel)**, a few miles away. You will pass through a gate on the way where you will be expected to pay a toll of a yuan or so. The Nine Bends Hotel is quite ugly and doesn't have much going for it except its location.

From there it is a quarter-mile walk (half of it straight up) to where you want to stay. Head beyond the food stalls and follow the main path. You'll see a long one-story building on your left. At the end of the building is a gate with a ticket table charging for access to the park grounds beyond. Pay the fee, get a little map and continue on through the ups and downs, ins and outs for a couple of minutes until you reach an open lawn with the river on your left. To your right two towering cliffs straddle the trail. The path leads between them, past a small hut, and to your left over a stream. Go up the path to your left. (Any really interesting place in China requires effort to get there.) By the time you get to the top of this cliff you will definitely have put yourself out — and made your China trip more memorable.

At the top is a handsome two-storey monastery set back behind a beautiful lawn. The monastery has a tea house and restaurant on the ground floor with 4 modest rooms encircled by a balcony forming the second. The showers are cold, the plumbing smelly, the rooms don't have heat, and the beds sag. On the other hand, the views are awe-inspiring and the misty mood puts you in touch with the culture of this ancient civilisation. A man in his 20s and his two younger siblings run the monastery and do a superb job of making you feel welcome. If you have a spirit of adventure, go for it.

In 1986 a room for three days with excellent meals and lots of beer came to a total of £20 ($30).

Exploring Wuyi Shan: At dawn there will be groups of Chinese on the ridges adjoining this little monastery. They climb up here to see the sunrise, which always draws the Chinese to mountaintops. No matter what summit you are on at first light, others will be there too. Most Chinese live on flat plains under hazy skies, so sunrise has become an art form. (It seems that every third painting or photo in China is titled 'Sunrise over ...') Your advantage is that, depending on which of the four rooms is yours, you can see the sunrise by sitting up in bed. The morning mist disappearing over the hills is the making of landscape paintings.

After breakfast, take an idyllic walk up the stream behind the hotel a short distance, then cross over and climb up to the little ridge. From there the trail descends through a gate and down a flight of stairs, then branches. The trail to the left will lead you back to the river much easier than if you take the one up the cliff face. This is the way to go and come from now on. Turn right and go though the fields following the main path. You will find a little monastery-type tea house much like the one where you are staying. Having some tea, follow the path toward the river for a few minutes and you'll come to a beautiful little gate. If any English-speaking Chinese tourists are around they can explain the legends of the spot. Then back to your place for lunch.

After lunch would be a good time to take a bamboo raft on a trip along the river. Purchase tickets at the booth on the grassy area you passed just before you began your climb up the hill. The price depends on whether you want a chair on the raft or not. After buying the ticket (about £3 ($5) for two, with chairs), you will be led over to a boatman who will load you onto his bamboo raft, pole it upstream for about 30 minutes, and then turn it around and let it drift downstream for about an hour while you sit back and create your own fantasies.

Land transportation back to the hotel is not included in the price, and most often you will be left to your own devices. This would be a good time to go on down to the town where you first got off the bus and make your reservations for whenever you are leaving.

Several spots around Wuyi Shan that are popular with Chinese tourists are shown on your local maps — but if you are here for just a day or two, don't bother. Enjoy your mountain top. Write some poetry. Take some photos. And eat lots of the mushrooms grown in these valleys and famous in Chinese cooking. Elsewhere a few dried ones cost a fortune; here you can have handfuls of fresh ones added to every dish for free. They deserve their reputation.

Leaving Wuyi Shan: Take the bus 3 hours north to Shangrao, departing at 6:00, 13:30 or 15:40. There may be some redeeming features to Shangrao but we don't know of any; we just try to get out quickly. The schedule on the wall of the Shangrao railway station is all in Chinese and probably won't make much sense. Using your timetable printed partly in English, work out where and when you want to go, then ask at the counter for a ticket by train number.

At least 12 trains daily go from Shangrao toward Hangzhou and Shanghai, but only one has a good connection with a bus from Wuyi Shan: Train 210, leaving Shangrao at noon (12:10) and arriving in Hangzhou at 20:19. Catch the early bus out of Wuyi Shan, or else you'll regret it when you arrive in Hangzhou late at night.

Or you can go to Fuzhou via Nanping and take a boat or plane to Hangzhou. The bus from Wuyi Shan to Nanping leaves around 7:00 to connect with the 10:17 train from Nanping, arriving in Fuzhou at 13:55. Another train leaves Nanping at 16:23, arriving in Fuzhou at 20:20. Check the boat schedule you got from CITS in Xiamen.

TOUR 5
HANGZHOU

Hangzhou (pop. 1m) is one of the most popular tourist spots in China. The city built around the famous West Lake has numerous places worth seeing. The lakeshore itself is inviting for evening promenades. If you give them an opportunity, Chinese holidaymakers will probably approach you to start a conversation. As fellow tourists, the kinship they feel with you makes them very open and interested in getting to know you.

Suggested Schedule

Depart for Hangzhou. (Scheduled departure times vary.)
Arrive in Hangzhou.
Check into your hotel.
Go for a stroll around the lake.

Transport arrangements

Because of the train schedules, when you first arrive in Hangzhou stay overnight. The next day, go out to Shaoxing and return here for a final day of sightseeing before proceeding on to Shanghai the following morning. (Train connections direct from Shaoxing would get you into Shanghai at an ungodly hour.)

Morning trains originating in Hangzhou depart at 7, 8, and 9 for the three hour trip to Shanghai.

Lodging

The **Wang Hu Hotel** (2 Huancheng Xi Road; Telex: 35003 WHBG CN) has a 24 hour booking service and with 356 rooms is large enough usually to have a room available. At £15 ($25) and upwards for a double the price is fair for their comfortable, though uninteresting, motel style rooms. Their breakfast buffet, including both western and Chinese cuisine, costs only £1.20 ($2) and could let you skip lunch. Remember that they stop serving early. Although both are near the lake, neither the Wang Hu nor the nearby, shabbier and less expensive **Huaquao (Overseas Chinese) Hotel** at 92 Hubin Road allows you to appreciate its atmosphere. The area they are in is commercial and crowded. Given your arrival hour, however, one of these might be your most convenient choice.

The **Hangzhou Hotel** (78 Beishan/Yuefen Road; Telex: CN 35005 and tel. 22921) will allow you to enjoy the atmosphere of the lake but at a high price. The rooms at £60 ($100) and upwards tend to be filled with tour groups. Bookings can be made through Shangri-la International. The Hangzhou is located in beautiful grounds on the north side of the lake.

Because it is West Lake (Xi Hu) that makes Hangzhou so special, the ideal place to stay would be in a hotel in this area. Some suggestions: The **Xihu (West Lake) Guesthouse**, tel. 26867, four buildings around a garden, is in the £30-£60 ($50-$100) range. The **Huagang Hotel** is less luxurious and less expensive. Farther inland on the same side at the **Zheijiang Guesthouse** (£30-£60 ($50-$100), with an indoor swimming pool), the **Liulang Guesthouse** (£20-£35 ($30-$60), traditional Chinese architecture) and the **Huajiashan Guesthouse** (£30-£60 ($50-$100), villa type rooms). There are many other hotels. Hangzhou is such a fast-developing tourist area that prices and quality can change unexpectedly.

Sightseeing highlights

● ● ● **West Lake (Xi Hu):** You can spend a full day on the lake taking boats from one group of island temples and pavilions to another. Boats are readily available at many points around the lake. The sequence of your stops will be determined by where you are staying. Before you start out make sure you have a copy of the Hangzhou tourist map which shows the location of the major guesthouses, tourist sights, and some of the more interesting restaurants. As you tour, decide where you want to eat lunch and dinner.

● **Lingyin Temple:** This is the most interesting Hangzhou sight away from the lake. If you go there, don't miss the smiling Buddha. To get there, take the public bus that goes west along the north side of the lake.

ITINERARY OPTION: Putuo Shan — Ningbo

Putuo Shan (Pu Island Monastery) is the smallest of the nine sacred mountains in China. Its lovely island location makes for a pleasant and relaxing excursion.

To get there, take an overnight boat from Shanghai. This not only offers a comfortable way to travel, but also saves the cost of a night in a hotel and allows you to meet fellow tourists who will be almost exclusively Chinese.

A visit to Putuo Shan means rearranging your itinerary. Because the only workable transportation leaves from Shanghai, you'll need to reverse a week of the tour, doing

Hangzhou

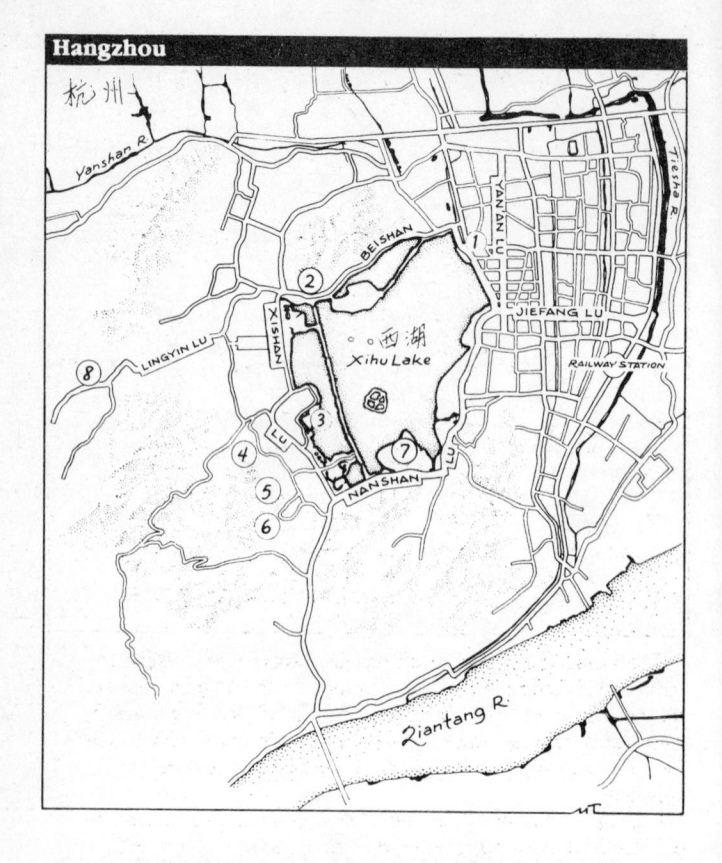

[Map of Hangzhou showing Xihu Lake, Yanshan R., Qiantang R., Beishan, Xishan, Nanshan, Lingyin Lu, Yan'an Lu, Jiefang Lu, Tiesha R., Railway Station, and numbered locations 1-8.]

Tours 9-11 of the main itinerary before Tours 6-8. You'll rejoin the main itinerary on Tour 13.

Food and lodging: There seems to be only one hotel for westerners to stay in Putuo Shan. It is located near the Puji Si pond. As you follow the crowds north away from the harbour, soon the pavement will end and a walkway will go off to the left. With the help of the locals, who will know where you are going even if you don't, you should reach the hotel in about 15 minutes.

The hotel, formerly a monastery, is quite satisfactory. It is possible (though difficult) to get good food in the hotel restaurant. Don't despair — Putuo Shan is filled with small restaurants that serve mouth-watering fresh seafood. Watch for people carrying basins of live crabs, and follow them to hole-in-the-wall restaurants where you can make a feast of them.

Tour 5

1.	望湖宾馆	Wang Hu Hotel
2.	杭州宾馆	Hangzhou Hotel
3.	西湖宾馆	Xihu Guesthouse
4.	浙江宾馆	Zheijiang Guesthouse
5.	六郎山宾馆	Liutong Guesthouse
6.	华家山宾馆	Huajiashan Guesthouse
7.	西子宾馆	Xizi Guesthouse
8.	林荫寺	Lingyin Temple

The island is small, permitting easy walks from temple to temple, with stops at beaches that attract the Chinese during the hot summers. They are pleasant beaches lovely for walks, with warm summer water for easy swimming, soft yellow sand for relaxing. If the weather is nice, the beaches will be crowded.

Pick up a map and find your way around. There are many old Buddhist buildings scattered over the island. Begin with Puyi Si, Fayu Si, Huiji Si (The syllable 'si' means 'temple') and Dacheng Monastery with its large reclining Buddha. Many of the temples are being reconstructed using traditional methods.

Departure: The afternoon hydrofoil to Ningbo takes less than two hours. An old ferry makes the same run and is cheaper, but it takes five hours.

Lodging (Ningbo): A short taxi or longer bus journey will get you to the Hua Qiao (Overseas Chinese) Hotel, one kilometre from the railway station. A double costs less than £15 ($20) and is quite posh. You can eat at the hotel, or at another nearby hotel with an outdoor cafe on a canal.

Sightseeing: Because you will have just a short morning in Ningbo you will want to take a taxi to see the lovely temples of Tiantong, Ayanwang and Bao Guo Si Temple.

Departure: In the early afternoon a train departs for Shaoxing which takes two hours. From there, transport back to Shanghai is the same as that described in 'Tours 6-8' of the main itinerary.

Putuo Shan Option Itinerary	
DAY 5	Depart Xiamen for Shanghai.
DAY 6	Sightseeing in Shanghai (see 'Tours 9 and 10' of the main itinerary).
DAY 7	Day or overnight trip tc Suzhou (see 'Tour 11' of the main itinerary).
DAY 8	Shanghai. Board the overnight boat to Putuo Shan.
DAY 9	Putuo Shan. Take the afternoon hydrofoil to the island of Ningbo, where you'll spend the night.
DAY 10	Morning in Ningbo. Afternoon train to Shaoxing. Spend the night in Shaoxing (see 'Tour 6' of the main itinerary).
DAY 11	Morning in Shaoxing. Travel to Hangzhou.
DAY 12	Hangzhou
DAY 13	Morning train to Shanghai (see 'Tour 8' of the main itinerary). Rejoin the main itinerary on 'Tour 13', noting the transport arrangements at the end of 'Tour 12'.

TOUR 6
SHAOXING

Shaoxing, an hour and ten minutes south of Hangzhou, is just far enough off the beaten track to be very special. What this town has, away from the main street, is quaintness: narrow lanes, twisting canals, many crafts, friendly people, an old Buddhist charity hospital for a hotel, and almost no tourists ... yet.

Suggested Schedule	
Early	Breakfast in Hangzhou either at your hotel or from the steamed bun vendors near the station.
8:20	Depart Hangzhou on early train for Shaoxing.
9:30	Upon arrival in Shaoxing, go to the Shaoxing Hotel and reserve crispy fish for lunch.
Morning	Wander Shaoxing's picturesque narrow streets and canals.
Lunch	Shaoxing Hotel.
Afternoon	Visit Emperor Yu Mausoleum.
Evening	Promenade on Main Street. Overnight in Shaoxing.

Transport
Shaoxing is an easy trip from Hangzhou. Take an 8:20 train out, arriving in Shaoxing at 9:30.

Pedicabs are at the railway station in Shaoxing. If you are going to the hotel, take one—it will be worth it. Otherwise, catch a bus across the street from the train station or walk into town. Either way takes about 10 minutes.

Sightseeing
The CITS office in Hangzhou has information available on what to see in Shaoxing. The ambience is what makes this town so inviting. Just meander and make an effort to get to the back streets. You can still hear the 'click click' of weaving looms as you wander through these narrow streets. Tracks down the source of the sounds and find yourself invited into small factories where people stop what they are doing to make a big show of welcoming you. This in contrast to many places in China where the signs say 'NO TOURISTS'.

• **Mt Fushan**, immediately behind the Shaoxing Hotel, is a nice place for an hour's walk. It can serve as your landmark to find the hotel.

Shaoxing

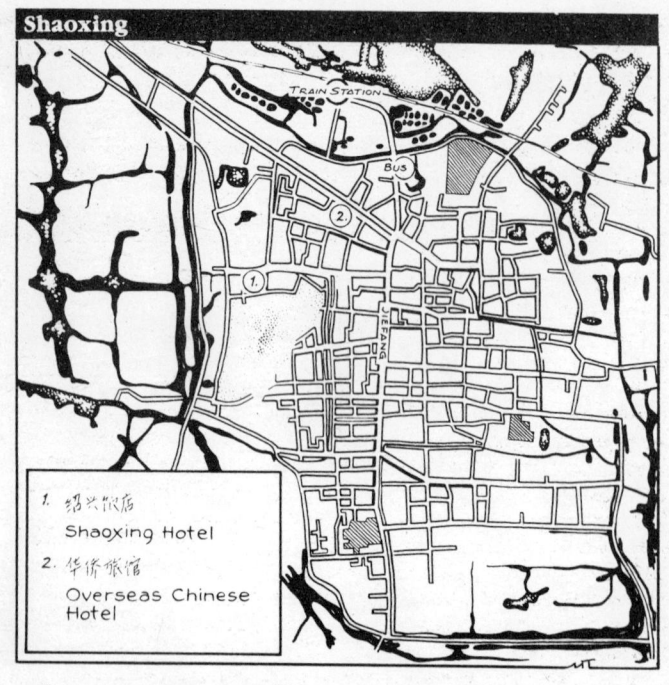

1. 绍兴饭店
   Shaoxing Hotel
2. 华侨旅馆
   Overseas Chinese Hotel

If you have time, you might want to take a Bus No. 2 from the centre of town to ●**Emperor Yu Mausoleum**, a few miles outside town. You can see all you want in 30 minutes. Bus No. 2 returns to the railway station.

Food

Plan on having lunch at the **Shaoxing Hotel** (not to be confused with the Overseas Chinese Hotel). Allow thirty minutes to walk there from the main street. It is less than six blocks away, but the side streets are so interesting that it can take a while to get there. The dining room isn't much for decor or service, and it definitely isn't the place for breakfast, but they do have the best crispy fish with sweet and sour sauce in China. Call at the restaurant and order it in advance, as they often run out. The head waitress speaks excellent English.

Take a look through the round doors at the old section of the hotel, once a Buddhist charity hospital. You will spend the night here and return to Hangzhou tomorrow. Adequate rooms cost £10 ($15) for a double with bath. At night Shaoxing's main street is still a walking street, with little motor traffic, many bicycles, and pleasant people.

TOUR 7
RETURN TO HANGZHOU

Your preference will determine whether you depart from Shaoxing for Hangzhou in the morning or the afternoon.

Suggested Schedule	
Breakfast	On the street, unless the hotel's western breakfast has improved recently.
Morning	Depart for Hangzhou. Overnight in Hangzhou.

Return transport to Hangzhou

Leave yourself ample time to get to the railway station. We didn't, on our first visit, and discovered that there was no taxi available. Luckily a friendly mule wagon got us there in time. Be prepared.

A train leaves Shaoxing at 10:40, to reach Hangzhou at 12:23. Later trains leave at 16:12, 21:00 and 21:37 and take about an hour to Hangzhou.

TOUR 8
SHANGHAI

An early morning departure will get you into Shanghai before noon, the perfect time to check into a hotel, allow you time to get organised, eat lunch and then wander this elegant city. End your day over a drink at the Jazz Club in the Peace Hotel.

Suggested Schedule	
Morning	Depart Hangzhou. (Trains leave Hangzhou at 7:00, 8:00 and 9:00 for the three-hour trip to Shanghai.)
Noon	Arrive in Shanghai (pop. 7m). Check into your hotel and have lunch.
Afternoon	Arrange onward transportation. Walking tour. Dinner. Jazz Club.

Arrival
Taxis in Shanghai are readily available and inexpensive. Take one to your hotel.

Ideally, you've made hotel reservations ahead of time (write to the hotel direct or ask a travel agent to help you; you probably won't be able to make the reservation from another city in China, but try anyway). If you were unable to do so, go directly to the Peace Hotel. The receptionists there are particularly helpful about suggesting or even phoning other hotels for you.

Lodging
As recently as 1985, it was nearly impossible to find a hotel room in Shanghai. In the half dozen hotels available then, most rooms were leased to foreign companies and not open to tourists. Thousands of new hotel rooms have been added recently to alleviate the problem. Several of the older hotels in Shanghai are owned and operated by what in western business circles would be called a conglomerate, running their own supply operations and transport, and frequently bypassing state-run enterprises.

We recommend the **Peace Hotel**, either the main Northern Building or the Southern Annex across the street with its separate registration and reception desk. (Conveniently located near the Bund: Northern Building, 20 Nanking Road, tel. 211244; Southern Building, 23 Nanking Road, tel. 218050.) They can often squeeze you in for a day or so even if they can't take you for longer because of advance bookings. At the upper end of the price range, around £25-£60 ($40-$100), the Northern Building usually has something available depending on the season; the Southern Annex is less luxurious, less renovated and less expensive. In the £15-£30 ($25-$50) category you will need luck, perseverance and/or reservations.

At the Peace Hotel, as in Hong Kong's YMCA, sooner or later you'll meet everyone travelling in China. The CITS office in the main lobby can arrange your tickets onward. The bar is a popular night spot, and the restaurant on the 8th floor is usually crowded.

Jinjiang Hotel at 59 Maoming Nan Road (720 units) has an air of European elegance. Formerly part of the French Club across the street, this hotel offered Europeans living in Shanghai amenities from home such as an indoor swimming pool, billiard room and bowling alley. Now the services are more basic: hotel with bars, restaurants and mini-supermarket. Service and maintenance are erratic and the price of a drink in the bar seems like a rip-off. The rooms, though, are comfortable. Prices are £45 ($80) and upwards.

The Jing'an Guest House, 370 Huashan Road, tel. 53-3050, about the same distance from the centre of town as the Jinjiang — a convenient taxi ride away. Colonial elegance, with a lovely garden and outdoor cafe, make it a pleasant place to stay. Though it may be booked up by tour groups or long term residents, it is worth checking whether they have a room.

Shanghai Mansions, 20 Suzhou North Road. Built in 1934, it was renovated in the mid 1980s. The rooms (motel modern) are noisy and uninspiring, but some have pleasant river and harbour views. The restaurants are good, though, like the rooms, not inviting.

Pujiang Hotel, across the street from the Shanghai Mansions, is the former Astor House Hotel, faded glamour from Shanghai's cosmopolitan days gone by. For years it has been the backpackers' special, though future renovation may change this. They offer every type of accommodation — from doubles with private bath at £10 ($15), to mattresses for £1 ($2) on the floor of a once-elegant indoor courtyard, with every bed-and-bath combination in between including dormitories for six to eight people. If you get stuck without a room in Shanghai, go to the Pujiang at 11:00 (check out time), review the **Mei you** section while waiting, and get yourself a bed for one night.

More hotel possibilities are the **Cypress Hotel** also known as the Longbai, and the familiar names of the **Shanghai Hilton**

Shanghai

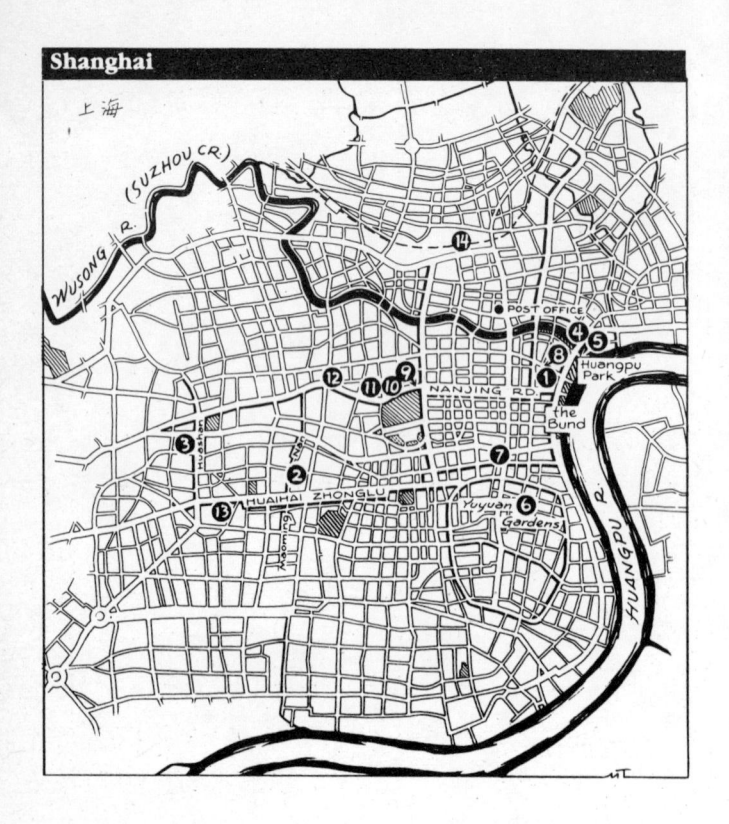

上海

and the **Shanghai Sheraton**, both easy places to make reservations because of their international networks. Dozens of other hotels are in the planning stages.

Several universities in Shanghai have guesthouses or private apartments for foreign lecturers, which are rented to the public when not in use. A friendly receptionist at a hotel registration desk may agree to phone around and help you find such a place.

Transport arrangements

Now is the time to make arrangements at the CITS desk in the Peace Hotel (Northern Building). This is one of the most organised and accommodating — albeit overworked — CITS offices in China. Don't be discouraged by the queues.

Purchase train tickets for Suzhou and tickets onward to Qufu or Beijing (see details in 'Tour 11').

1. 和平饭店   Peace Hotel
2. 锦江宾馆   Jinjiang Hotel
3. 静安宾馆   Jing'an Guesthouse
4. 上海大厦   Shanghai Mansions
5. 黄浦公园   Huangpu Park
6. 豫园   Yuyuan Gardens
7. 上海博物馆   Shanghai Museum
8. Friendship Store
9. Park Hotel
10. Shanghai Arts and Crafts
11. Acrobatic Theater
12. Friendship Store (Antiques)
13. Conservatory of Music
14. Shanghai Railway Station

Sightseeing

The travel logistics involved will probably mean you'll spend a combination of partial days and full days in Shanghai. Our sightseeing recommendations can be abbreviated or expanded as necessary to fit into your schedule. Whereas in Beijing we will suggest you see every temple and historic monument your feet can handle, Shanghai lends itself better to street wandering and store browsing. Shanghai has the best organised post office for sending parcels from China (see 'Staying in touch' at the front of this book), and many shops carry merchandise appealing to western standards and tastes. In other words, it is a good place to buy.

If you are staying in the Peace Hotel or another hotel in the same vicinity, it is easy to fit these activities in when you have a few hours available.

Shanghai sightseeing and shopping excursion 1

● ● **Huangpu Park** and the ● ● **Bund** lend themselves to both early morning and late evening sitting and strolling. The Bund has been a favourite promenade spot since the early part of this century when Shanghai was known as 'the Paris of the Orient'. Huangpu Park is the place to watch elderly Chinese doing tai chi at dawn. They welcome foreigners to join and especially enjoy seeing people who come back day after day. It's a good way to meet people. Earlier in the lifetimes of some of these agile old gentlemen, they would have been confronted at the park entrance by a sign dating from the British colonial era (the park was established in 1868) reading 'NO DOGS OR CHINESE ALLOWED'. Huangpu Park is open from 5:00 to 22:00.

The **Friendship Store**, recently relocated to a large building about a three to four minute walk behind the Peace Hotel, carries a vast array of goods worth looking at. If you are looking for a bottle of Great Wall White Wine this is the place to find it.

Evening

This has probably been a tiring day. Treat yourself to an early dinner on the 8th floor of the Peace Hotel, followed by a drink at the **Jazz Club** downstairs, a trip into a 1940s time warp. The musicians learned to play jazz from westerners during those years, but were not allowed to play during the Cultural Revolution. Now they play happily every night. Look ... isn't that Bogie and Bacall at the next table?

TOUR 9
SHANGHAI

A stroll along streets filled with bookshops and calligraphy supplies leads to the Shanghai Museum, which offers an introduction to the richness of traditional Chinese art.

Suggested Schedule	
Breakfast	At your hotel or have a cutlet at the 'Austrian' Deda Cafe, corner of Nanjing Road and Sichuan Road (see 'Tour 10' excursion).
Morning	Walk toward the Shanghai Museum, following your map and stopping in shops along the way.
Afternoon	Visit the museum.
Dinner	Cantonese dinner (early) at the Xin Ya Restaurant.

Shanghai sightseeing and shopping excursion 2

Set out in the direction of the **Shanghai Museum**. You can visit several good shops on the way to this outstanding art museum. A foreign language bookshop carries a good selection of books in English and other languages, maps, original art work and reproductions, and children's books that make wonderful gifts. On the same street are several Chinese language bookshops that also carry recorded music. Two or three nice little places carry calligraphy supplies. One shop has a large supply of traditional cotton cloth-soled black shoes which have been replaced in most of China by plastic horrors.

The museum, with its wonderful collection of original artwork, should be visited when you have enough time to linger. Take a quick walk through the three-storey building for an overall view, then return to enjoy the exhibits that interest you most at leisure. Recheck the hours before starting off. The museum is usually open 9:00 to 17:00, but it's closed Mondays, lunch times, some mornings especially in summer and, we suspect, whenever they see you coming.

There's no better way to end a day in Shanghai than with a promenade along the Bund.

For a delicious early dinner, ask your hotel receptionist to reserve you a table at the **Xin Ya Restaurant**, 719 Nanjing Dong Road, tel. 223636, 226085.

TOUR 10
SHANGHAI

Today is a day to stroll, shop and become acquainted with some of Shanghai's older, more elegant areas.

Suggested Schedule	
Breakfast	At your hotel.
Morning	Set out down Nanjing Road.
Lunch	At the vegetarian restaurant near the Park Hotel.
Afternoon	In the French Section and Yuyuan Gardens. Return to Peace Hotel for dinner.

Shanghai sightseeing and shopping excursion 3

Today's excursion route forms a large rectangle bounded at its four corners by the Peace Hotel, the Antique and Curio Shop on Nanjing Road, the Jinjiang Hotel, and the Yuyuan Gardens. This route provides an excellent one day overview of Shanghai.

From the Peace Hotel, go up along Nanjing Road. One of the first interesting shops (on a corner a couple of blocks down on the right) carries traditional Chinese musical instruments. Further down, on a corner across the street, a small shop window displays opera costumes. Inside the shop there is no sign of them, but if you go to the rear and up the narrow stairway you'll find a marvellous costume shop that can outfit you for many fancy dress parties to come.

The nearby **Deda Cafe**, an 'Austrian' coffee shop, serves veal cutlets, ice cream sundaes, cakes, pies, and other things that look good but lack flavour.

Crossing back to the right side of the street, you will come to several silk shops and a large art shop that sells calligraphy supplies on the ground floor and artwork on the second. On the same side is a fan shop; even if you don't want to buy, it is interesting to observe the importance given to selecting the proper silk or paper fan.

Half a mile after setting out you will pass the Park Hotel, and just beyond that, the Shanghai Arts & Crafts Shop. Behind the shop, tucked almost in an alley, is a marvellous vegetarian restaurant. To reach it, go right at the corner where you see the Arts & Crafts Shop until you come to the back of the block. On the left is what looks like a food canteen with people picking up their food at the counter. Walk through that room to swinging doors in the back and enter another rather attractive restaurant with dark wood panelling that continues for several rooms. Find yourself a table with people who look friendly enough to help you order, since the menu is only in Chinese. (Or you can point.) If you don't enjoy vegetarian food, eat at the Park Hotel, where the restaurant decor is not inviting, but the food is good.

After lunch take a look around the **Shanghai Arts & Crafts Shop**. On the third floor they carry a good selection of silk carpets.

At this point you might want to catch a taxi at the Park Hotel and go on to the Jinjiang. Or you can continue on down Nanjing Road to the **Acrobatic Theatre**, where you can find out about tickets for an evening performance. If you have trouble getting tickets (sometimes they are all reserved for tour groups), right before the performance you can usually find Chinese selling tickets that they have been allocated. The Acrobatic Theatre is intended as 'tour group entertainment', and most individual travellers find better ways to use their time.

If you are interested in antiques, the **Friendship Store Antique and Curio Branch** is further down on the same side of the street. Nearby is a pleasant tree lined area of the old French Section, where you should be able to get a taxi to the Jinjiang Hotel. From the hotel, walk on south to the next street where you'll come to Huaihai Shonglu, another major east-west street. Turn right. A few blocks will bring you to the **Conservatory of Music**, 15 minutes beyond is the **United States Consulate**. Both are lovely old French complexes.

The other direction has more shops. When you get tired of them, get a taxi (sometimes it takes a while on this street) and go to the Yuyuan Gardens.

The **Yuyuan Gardens** were laid out in 1537. One hundred years ago some merchants purchased part to create a shopping area which became the most popular in Shanghai. Located in the old Chinese quarter of the city, the buildings are relatively unchanged. For eating there are many tasty food stands and the popular **Old Shanghai Restaurant**.

From here it is a short taxi ride or a 30 minute walk along the Bund back to the Peace Hotel.

TOUR 11
SUZHOU

Suzhou's gardens are among the most inspiring man-made environments in the world. These gardens served as the models for the Zen gardens in Kyoto and Nara, Japan. They can be mystical and magical, or crowded and noisy, depending on when you are there. The gardens (there are several significant ones) are best visited early in the morning or late in the evening shortly before they close. At midday the chaos of untold numbers of people jostling each other and clambering over beautiful rock formations to have their pictures taken is a sight better left unseen.

Suggested Schedule

Early Morning	Depart from Shanghai. arrive in Suzhou (pop. 600,000).
Afternoon	Visit the gardens of Suzhou.
Evening	Overnight in Suzhou OR return to Shanghai on the early evening train for a better connection to Qufu.

Getting there

A commuter train leaves Shanghai at 6:06 in the morning, arriving in Suzhou at 7:26. There are also trains at 5:00, 5:22 and 6:50, each taking about an hour and ten minutes. The easiest one to get a seat on is the 6:06 commuter train. If you are going on to Qufu by night train, deposit your luggage at the station. Should you plan to stay the night in Suzhou, take a taxi directly to the Master of the Nets Garden to be there at an early hour. Ask them to hold your luggage at the gate.

Suzhou day tour

● ● ● The **Master of the Nets Garden** has a tea house frequented by elderly Chinese men enjoying their morning tea and smoke. Be here at 7:30 when it opens and the beauty and tranquillity of these gardens will be yours forever. Have a cup of tea in an out of the way spot where you can view a favourite part of the gardens and the tea drinkers. The purpose of a place like this will become evident.

Have some breakfast if necessary and then head for the **Surging Wave Pavilion** (Canlangting). It is twenty minutes on foot (see map). On the way, experience the quaintness of these little streets with the arched bridges over the canals. After you finish here, take Bus No. 1 headed back towards the railway station and get off in the middle of town, at Renmin Lu and

Tour 11

Suzhou

1. 网师园 — Master of the Nets Garden
2. 沧浪亭 — Canglangting Garden
3. 苏州饭店 — Suzhou Hotel
4. 南林 — Nanlin Hotel
5. 姑苏宾馆 — Gusu Hotel
6. 留院 — Liuyuan Garden
7. 拙政园 — Zhuozheng Garden

Guanquian, or you can walk it in 20 minutes. There are many lunch type restaurants in this area including several dumpling places up the street to the east. After lunch and shopping in some of the silk shops, there are two options. One is to take Bus No. 5 to the **Liuyuan Gardens** and return. The other is to carry on up the main street to the **North Temple** either on foot or on Bus No. 1. You can climb this nine-storey pagoda for good views of the town. After leaving here take a walk to **Zhuozheng Garden** and the nearby **Suzhou Museum**. Once a private residence, the museum offers historic information to complete your image of Suzhou.

By now it is almost time to head back to the Master of the Nets Garden for late afternoon tea and some rest before having dinner at one of the restaurants in the **Suzhou Bazaar** (get there early).

Suzhou is so charming that you could easily stay several days. The area around the Grand Canal and the lake is level and lends itself to long-distance bicycle riding. Most of the companies that offer bicycle tours in China concentrate their trips on the area around Suzhou and Wuxi. You can hire a bicycle near the Suzhou Hotel.

Lodging

Three hotels, clustered together, are approximately equal in cost. They are the **Suzhou Hotel**, the **Guzhou Hotel** and the **Nanlin Hotel**. The Suzhou, 15 Shinquan Jie, tel. 4616, has the tourist amenities — theatre, Friendship Store, etc.

Wuxi option

The next town further out is Wuxi, a pleasant town on the lake within easy distance of Shanghai. During the years when there was a hotel shortage in Shanghai, travellers could stay in Wuxi and commute to Shanghai for business or pleasure. Large tour groups occasionally usurp all the hotel space in Suzhou, forcing individual travellers on to Wuxi.

In the spring, lovely bonsai displays coincide with the blossoming of fruit trees to create a wonderful time for you — and twenty million other people. In spite of the crowds, it is worth a visit during that time of the year.

There are three inexpensive (£10-£15 ($15-$20)) hotels clustered together out of town on Lake Taihu where tour groups get bused, and it is usually easy enough to find a room.

Leaving Suzhou

When you leave Suzhou you will be going toward Beijing with a stop in the wonderful little town of Qufu. Access to Qufu is by bus from the railway station at Yanzhou half an hour away.

There are two choices for getting to Yanzhou from Suzhou. One is to return to Shanghai and take Train No. 156, which departs from Shanghai at 18:52. This train passes through

Suzhou at 19:56, so if you have made your reservations you can pick it up here and avoid backtracking to Shanghai. The reservation, even in this case, should be made from Shanghai (the train's departure point) so you can get a reserved seat instead of just a ticket; it's sometimes hard to reserve seats en route. The train arrives in Yanzhou at 8:00 the following morning. Cost is £15 ($25) for a soft sleeper. The other choice is Train No. 110, which originates in Suzhou and departs at 21:36, arriving in Yanzhou at 9:25. The deciding factor is ticket availability.

Should you decide to bypass Qufu, there are four flights daily from Shanghai to Beijing, taking less than two hours and costing about £30 ($50).

TOUR 12
QUFU

Qufu, Confucius' birthplace, is among our favourite places in China. Since it's not easy for large groups of people to get to and from, Qufu remains a pleasant, relaxed small town with a rural atmosphere and friendly cheerful locals. The Chinese plan to develop it into a major tourist attraction, airport and all, so the quaintness has a time limit.

Suggested Schedule

Morning	Arrive, check into Confucian Mansions, make travel arrangements to Taian. Visit Temple of Confucius. Lunch at hotel.
Afternoon	Pedicab to Confucian Forest.

Transport
Leave from Shanghai at 18:52 Train No. 156, arriving in Yanzhou at 8:08. (See 'Leaving Suzhou' in Tour 11 for alternatives.) Across the road from the station will be several waiting buses. Find the one going to Qufu (pronounced 'chu fu') and hop on for the 20-minute ride.

Lodging
The place to stay in Qufu is the **Confucian Mansions,** an easy walk or pedicab ride from the bus station. Taking a pedicab makes finding the entrance easier. Most maps make the entrance appear to be off the main street, but in fact it is off a side street about a block west of the main tower. The Confucian Mansions was the residence of 77 consecutive generations of Confucius. The chain was only broken in 1948 when the direct heir fled to Taiwan. A double with bath costs about £7 ($11).

Most of the buildings in the Confucian Mansions were rebuilt during the Ming and Qing dynasties. The plumbing, unfortunately, seems sometimes to be almost that old. But it is worth a little discomfort to wake up in the morning to have your coffee (if you've brought your own) in those lovely courtyards.

Get settled into your room. If you intend to go to Taian, make arrangements with the receptionist at the hotel to purchase your bus ticket. They will do so for a little, if any, markup over what it would cost you to buy it yourself. By now it is time for lunch in the hotel dining room. After eating, you're off to see the town.

Qufu

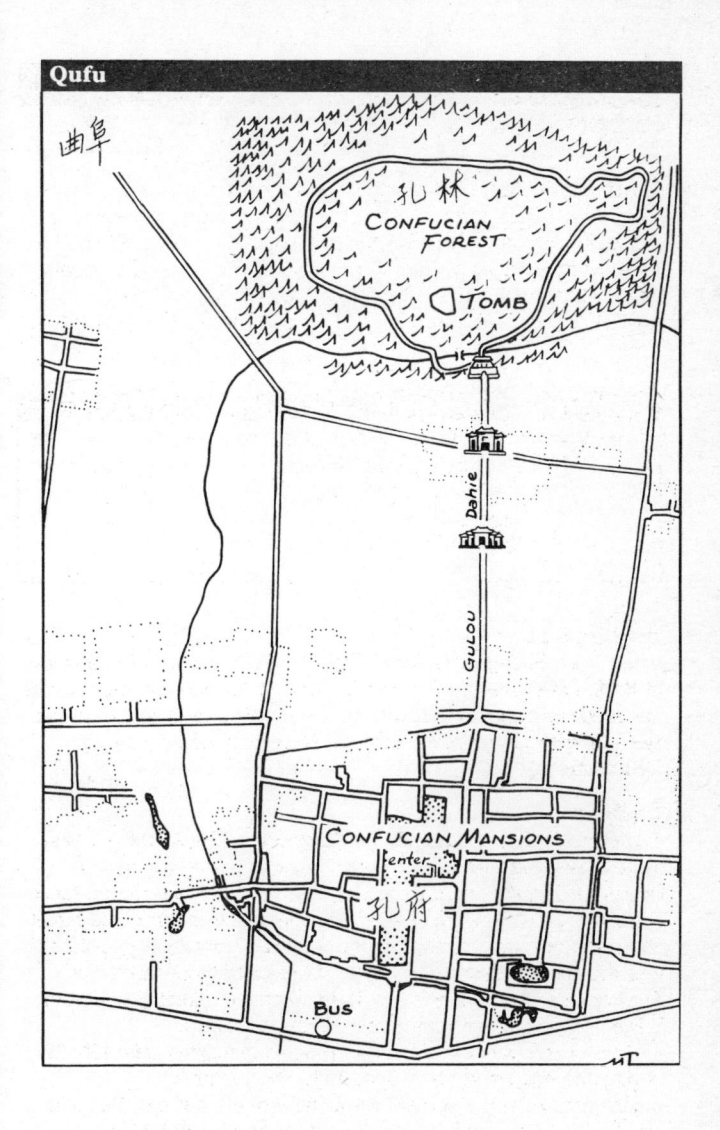

Sightseeing highlights
Confucius, whose Chinese name is Kong Fu Zi (Master Kong), was born in Qufu in 551 BC. For most of his life he wandered the country seeking a prince who would follow his rules of

government. In his last years of life he returned to Qufu to teach a large contingent of disciples until his death in 479 BC. One year later, Duke Ai of Lu transformed his house into a temple and during all the following centuries over 70 generations of Confucius' family lived in what became known as the Confucian Mansions. 20% of the town's population still claim to be descendants of Confucius. Those in direct line still receive pensions from the state and therefore have no need to work.

A pedicab is a wonderful way to see this small town.

● ● ● **The Temple of Confucius** is so rich and vast that you should allow several hours to see it. If there is any time before lunch, wander in for a short visit and return later. ● ● **The Confucian Forest** is a 500-acre man made forest. Disciples of Kong Fu Zi planted the forest with thousands of trees brought from all over China. As you wander through the forest, you'll find hundreds of elaborate tombs and statues. Confucius and all of his descendants are buried here.

There are numerous other sites in and around town, but if you are only going to be there for a day it is best to spend the remainder of your time in the sprawling Mansions. They go on and on, and if you don't check the maps (available locally) you may think you have seen it all when in reality you haven't even got to the main part.

TOUR 13
TAI SHAN

Tai Shan is the most revered and popular of China's sacred mountains. Sunrise from its peak is a fabled sight, the subject of paintings and verse throughout China's history.

Suggested Schedule

Morning	Awake in Qufu.
	Take the morning bus to Taian.
	Go to the minibus for the cable car, buy ticket, eat lunch (if time permits).
Afternoon	Take the cable car to the mountaintop.
	Sleep on top, or in town at the Taishan Guest House, or catch the night train on to Beijing.

Getting there

Take a morning bus from Qufu. The two-hour journey will cost a pound or so. You will be let off near the railway station in the town of Taian. (See map.) About two blocks from there is a minibus station, with frequent departures, that will take you most of the way up Tai Shan. At the end of the minibus route, a cable car will lift you up to the top of the mountain. You can avoid waiting in the queue for the cable car if you are willing to pay more.

Lodging

You can stay either on the mountain or in Taian.

Taishan Guest House (tel. 4694) is located in town at the beginning of the trail. It is an uninteresting but adequate hotel; doubles cost around £10 ($15). The CITS desk is in the lobby. It is open at odd hours — be persistent. The restaurant is unappetising.

Zhong Tian (meaning 'Halfway Gate to Heaven') **Guest House** is at the cable car departure point. The price is less than the Taishan, and it is less comfortable.

Daiding Guest House is at the summit. It's down-to-basics, inexpensive, and the only place to stay if you want to see the sunrise. Eat at any of the hotels or the many food stands on the way up the mountain, none of them particularly noteworthy.

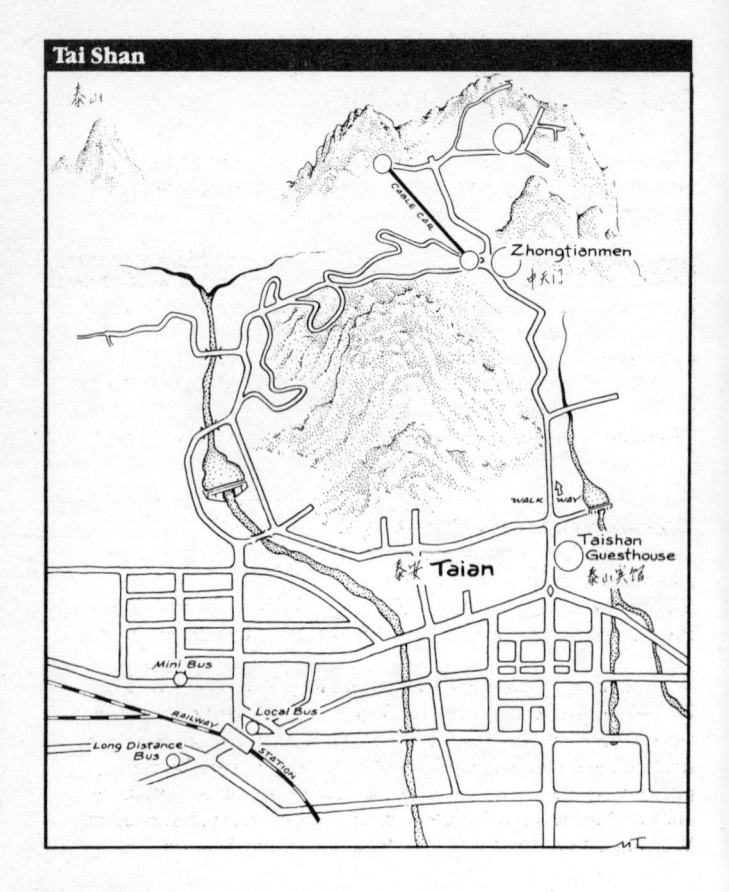

Tai Shan

Tai Shan, situated in the heart of China's most populated region, midway between Shanghai and Beijing, attracts masses of people and so does not permit the private meditative experience that travellers may find at China's other sacred mountains. The temples and shrines with Taoist, Buddhist and Confucian influences will make your visit memorable.

Tai Shan is the only sacred mountain where you can ride to the top. You can also climb the mountain from the town below. Steps lead up to the cable car station. The pretty walk takes about three hours. In the peak tourist seasons, though, the walkway is packed with thousands of souvenir stands and tourists. If your time is limited, we recommend that you take a minibus or cable car to the top.

TOUR 14
TAI SHAN TO BEIJING

Chinese tradition says the day begins on Tai Shan. If you've spent the night at the summit, you can watch it happen.

Suggested Schedule	
Sunrise	On the mountaintop, or walking the lower trails if you've spent the night in town.
Morning	Depart for Beijing (OR Spend the day on the mountain and the night on the evening train to Beijing).
Evening	Arrive in Beijing. Dinner at the hotel and to bed — you'll be tired.

Transport to Beijing
Taian is one of the more confusing rail stations in China, so allow plenty of time to find your way around.

Four trains stop between 9:00 am and noon. All arrive in Beijing the same evening. (You'll find hotel information in 'Tour 15'.)

If you want to leave Taian in the evening; Train No. 126 stops in Taian at 22:26 and reaches Beijing at 7:10 the next morning. No sleepers are set aside for passengers boarding at Taian — all they can sell you is a hard seat ticket. Wait on the boarding platform for carriage No. 8, where the conductor is. Locate him and get him to upgrade your ticket to sleeper accommodation. You might have to wait a few stops until a berth is vacated.

TOUR 15
BEIJING

This will be a long, exciting day. After arrival in Beijing (pop. 9m), energy permitting, you will see some of the city's most inspiring monuments, do some shopping, and finish your day at the opera.

Suggested Schedule	
Morning	Awaken in Beijing OR Arrive in Beijing early morning.
	Breakfast at hotel.
	Tiananmen Square.
Afternoon	Forbidden City.
	Shopping on Wang Fu Jing.
Evening	Chinese opera.

Arrival in Beijing
Beijing (formerly known as Peking) is a very large city and taxis are not expensive. All cabs have meters that are easy to read. Prices will vary according to elegance of the vehicle. Our suggestion is to take cabs or minibuses that go along main bus routes but will only stop where passengers want. They hustle to get occupants, so you will notice them.

Several Beijing streets change their names from segment to segment. The one that visitors will use most is the main east-west thoroughfare that goes past Tiananmen Square. It undergoes several name changes.

Lodging
The following hotels have convenient locations, fair prices, comfort, and a feel of being in China:

Beijing Hotel on Chang'an Dong Avenue Telex 42626,27,28CPL CN, has close to 1000 rooms, 20 dining areas offering varied cuisines, and shops, making this the preferred hotel for many long-term foreign residents and repeat China visitors who appreciate little conveniences such as a restaurant open until midnight and a cafe that serves croissants in the morning. Doubles are £30 ($50) in the New Wing, £30-£40 ($55-$70) in the old. The large rooms make a first impression of old world elegance; close scrutiny reveals signs of poor maintenance. The Chinese restaurant to the right on the main floor serves an excellent lunch with a certain amount of style. The Sichuan restaurant, also on the main floor, is good. The

Japanese restaurant is fine but quite expensive, and the western restaurant is not recommended by anyone we know.

Min Zu (National Minorities) Hotel, beyond the Forbidden City on the central thoroughfare at 51 Fuxingmennei (tel. 658541, telex 22991), is well-situated next to the Minorities Museum, and it is where the minority people stay when they are in town. (China's population is 93.3% Han people; the other 6.7% — 67 million people — belong to the 55 'Minority Nationalities' as the Chinese call them.) Don't expect hordes of exotic crowds. Minorities are rarely spotted in Beijing. The hotel offers 500 rooms on 11 floors, yet has a small homey feeling. The dining tooms, cafe, and lobby are pleasant and welcoming. The large restaurant on the main floor has enjoyable lunches. The rooms are attractive, well maintained and worth the £25 ($40) for a double. The staff is particularly friendly, helpful, and efficient.

Bamboo Gardens, at 24 Xiao Shi Qiao, is our favourite for external atmosphere with two storey buildings situated around a lovely oriental garden with the feel of a rich residence. The rooms, however, are basic motel modern, maintenance is poor and the rooms sometimes smell musty. It is not conveniently located and taxis are hard to come by from there. The staff is pleasant and personable and the garden restaurant is pretty enough to stop by for lunch. Doubles are in the £10-£30 ($20 -$50) range.

Jian Quo (tel. 595261), at the east end of the central thoroughfare where the name has changed to Jianguomenwai Dajie east of the Friendship Store. It is a preferred place to stay for those who demand high western standards. Unlike the Great Wall Hotel, it is centrally located. Operated by the Peninsula Group from Hong Kong, the hotel's service and maintenance are admirable. Every amenity is offered: relaxing main lobby bar, coffee bar, shops selling ham and cheese, pizza nights (Tuesday and Thursday) in the back restaurant, and other restaurants that cater to varying tastes. Doubles are in the £60 ($100) range.

Zhaolong Hotel (tel. 5002299, telex 210079 ZLh CN) is a tower on the east side of town near the stadiums and exhibition halls. It is not as well located for tourists and we'd rate it as a cheaper version of the above at £40 ($70) per double. Just a name to remember if you get stuck.

The **Hua Du** (tel. 50-1166, telegram 5431, telex 22028 HUADU CN) has an amusing quality. With plastic grape arbours and more, it is Chinese decor at its silliest. The rooms, service and food are more than adequate, worth the £15 ($28) for a double, but it is rather far from the centre of the city. Many tour groups stay here.

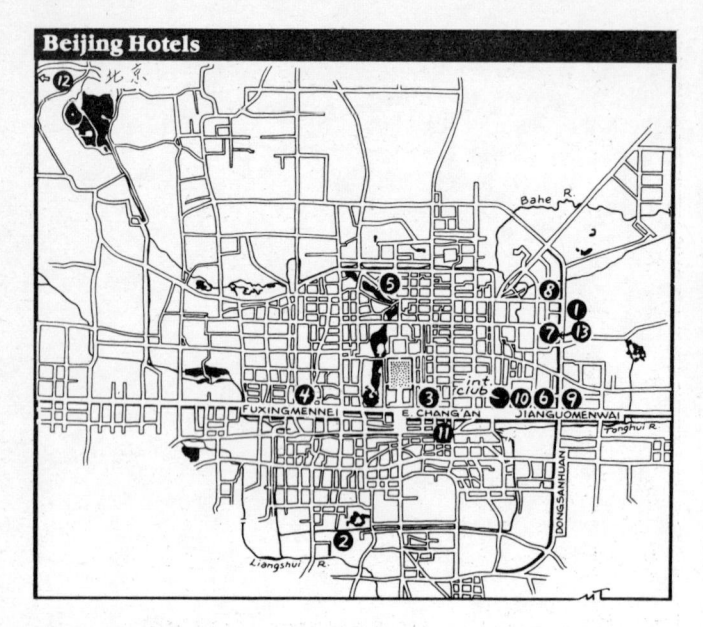

Beijing Hotels

Other Hotels:
The **Great Wall**, with its great prices of £60 ($100) and upwards per double, was modelled after a hotel in Dallas. Except for concessions to Chinese decor, it might just as well be in Texas. You may want to have a look at China's top of the line hotel accommodation as a standard for comparison. It is about 20 minutes from the centre of Beijing.

At the other extreme, at £5 ($8) per double, the **Qiao Yuan** (also twenty minutes from the centre of town) is where budget travellers from every part of the globe stay. In all our years of travel, never have we seen such a variety of nationalities in one place. It's an excellent place to gather information for this or future journeys. The Qiao Yuan's outdoor bar, a rare amenity in China, is packed nightly with travellers who regale each other with stories of the road. This hotel is operated under contract with CITS, so if you turn up at the desk they will send you to a CITS office. In 1986 the office was in Room 301, where we met Mr. Yue Xiong, one of the most helpful CITS people in China. Minibus tours operate from this hotel daily. Beijing offers so much to do that you are unlikely to be in your hotel room very much, so a basic hotel room may be all you want. Service here is minimal.

Naturally, there are many more hotels in Beijing. Here are a few that are *not* on our preferred list:

Tour 15

1.	长城	Great Wall Hotel
2.	华侨饭店	Qiao Yuan
3.	北京饭店	Beijing Hotel
4.	民族饭店	Min Zu Hotel
5.	竹园饭店	Bambu Gardens
6.	建国饭店	Jian Quo
7.	兆龙饭店	Zhaolong Hotel
8.	华都饭店	Hua Du Hotel
9.	光华饭店	Guan Hua Hotel
10.	友谊商店	Friendship Store
11.	新桥宾馆	Xin Qiao Hotel
12.	香山饭店	Xiangshan Hotel
13.	北京烤鸭店	Beijing Kao Ya Dian

Guan Ghua Hotel is a CITS operated hotel and in order to book it you must go through the CITS office located in the Chongwenmen Hotel. At £10 ($15) for a double the rooms are cheap, but it is a dreary place far from the centre and is mostly frequented by Chinese, though the staff does speak English.

The Friendship Hotel is a huge complex built for the Soviet experts and now used to house other foreigners working in Beijing. It has few rooms available for tourists and is far from town. Doubles, if there are any, £15-£20 ($25-$30).

Xin Qiao Hotel has all of the advantages of the Min Zu but is presently exclusively Japanese or at least no one else seems to get in. They have a lovely restaurant on the top floor with excellent food and some of the most refined service we have experienced in China.

Xiangshan (Fragrant Hills) Hotel is not well situated for visiting the city proper, located as it is over an hour from town. But it is a wonderful site for wandering in rural China. Designed by I.M. Pei in 1982, poor construction and management have brought the hotel to sad times. Reports are that improvements are being made and discounts are offered in off season, but who would want to be out here in mid winter?

The Peace Hotel was merely a hole in the ground the last time we saw it. It may be finished by now, but then again, it may not. Large numbers of hotels are in various stages of planning or construction in Beijing and the government will speed up or slow down the process according to the need for rooms.

Food

Many of the best restaurants are located in the hotels mentioned above. At the end of a day amidst Beijing's overwhelming crowds you may be very content to retreat to your hotel for a quiet dinner. The restaurants in the **Beijing**, **Min Zu** and **Xin Qiao** hotels are worth seeking out. The **Bamboo Gardens** has a pleasant outdoor atmosphere but it is not noted for its food. The **Jian Quo** offers a variety of restaurants serving western fare and an elegant, expensive Chinese restaurant.

The **CITIC Building**, visible from all over Beijing, has a Chinese luncheon buffet on the 28th floor for £5 ($8). Dinner is also served here — try the Peking duck. On the 29th floor is a western restaurant. Both eating areas offer a soothing ambience and inspiring views of the city. Their food is excellent, though notoriously expensive.

The **International Club** has both a restaurant and a coffee shop. The food is tasty, the price fair, and it is a good place to meet foreigners living in Beijing. Nearby is the **Friendship Store**, with a delicatessen and a supermarket where travellers stop for bread, ham, cheese, and a drink. It is a good place to stock up on your picnic supplies for day excursions out of Beijing, and also to gather information.

Beijing has a vast number of restaurants that serve Peking duck. Most of them are unimaginatively named **Beijing Roast Duck Restaurant (Beijing Kao Ya Dian)**. Our favourite restaurant by that name is a small one around the corner from the Zhao Long Hotel on Dong San Huan Beilu, on the southeast corner of the intersection with Gon Gren Ti Yu Chang Beijie. Collect a group of fellow travellers and get to the restaurant early enough to be sure of getting a table. It is open for lunch from 11:00 to 14:00 and dinner from 17:00 to 22:00.

Ritan Restaurant in Ritan Park, with its pleasant outdoor eating area, is a favourite of long-term foreign residents.

Tiananmen Square Area

天安门广场

GUGONG

TIAN'ANMEN SQUARE

WANG FU JING

E. CHANG'AN

GUGONG (Forbidden City) 故宫 (紫禁城)
1. Beijing Hotel

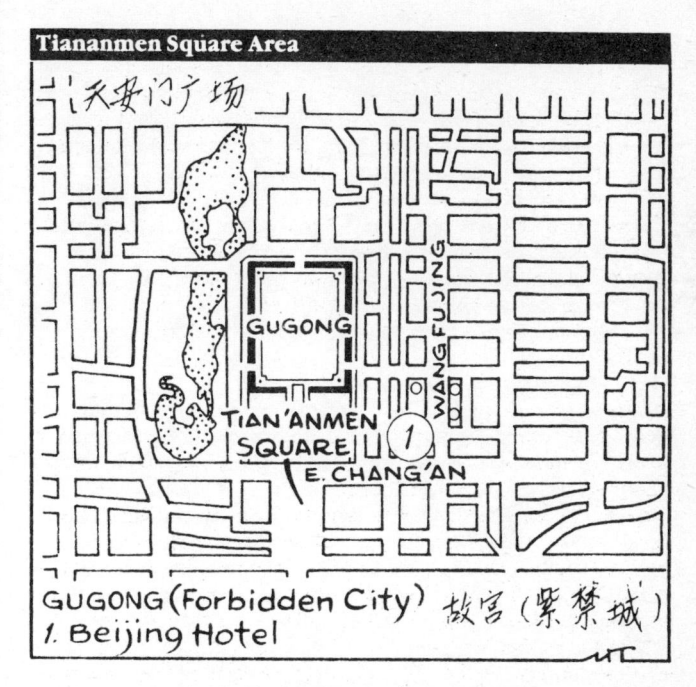

There are many good restaurants with speciality foods from all over China. Fellow travellers and long-term residents are your best source of information in choosing where to eat.

Beijing walking tour

We suggest you eat a hearty breakfast and prepare a snack to take along. Today's walking tour offers scant opportunities for eating until late afternoon. Over breakfast, study a guide and map of the Imperial Palace and plan your strategies. Here are some suggestions.

Take a taxi to Tiananmen Square, where any visit to Beijing should begin, for the city revolves around this square. Its vast 98 acre expanse gives a stark visual image of China's immense population. Some sites hold the presence of the masses even when they are empty, and Tiananmen Square is one of them. Walk to the Gu Gong (Forbidden City).

Three parallel walkways go from north to south. The central one is the most dramatic and important, so walk down this one first and save the others for your way back out.

Passing through the various gates and hallways that run through the centre of the city can take more than an hour. The exhibition halls are in the buildings to the rear. Take a look at each — there are buildings filled with hundreds of magnificent clocks, bronzes, jewellery, ceramics — the treasures of a civilisation. Though not always well displayed, the quality and variety is extraordinary.

Around lunch time, plan on being in the area of the Imperial Garden, where you can get a soft drink.

The living quarters of the royal family, particularly the western palaces where the empress and the concubines resided, are in excellent condition and give a slight idea of the grandeur this complex once had. There will often be special exhibits at a small extra fee, usually worth it.

By now you should be ready to sit down. Head for the Beijing Hotel by taxi for a cup of coffee or a drink depending on your mood. If you still have energy after this rest, go left out of the hotel and left again at the first street, Wang Fu Jing. Within a block you'll come to a large bookshop, with art books and maps on the 3rd floor. Down the block on the same side at No. 200 is the Beijing Arts and Crafts Store, with a good selection at much better prices than the Friendship Store. Almost directly across the street is the Beijing Huaxia Arts and Crafts Store (also known as the Theatre Shop) with an area upstairs for antiques and old clothing. It looks like an antique shop should: old, dusty and musty.

By now it is time for dinner and then the opera.

Sightseeing highlights

● ● ● **Tiananmen Square (Gate of Heavenly Peace):** 20th Century Chinese history can be traced by events that took place here. Tiananmen Square did not exist during the time of the empire. Government buildings lined the way from Tian an men Gate to Zheng yang men Gate. At the end of the last century some of the buildings were damaged and later destroyed. After the fall of the empire the new government used the former Imperial Palace for a short time, so the square became the natural place for demonstrations. On May 4, 1919, the Treaty of Versailles, which gave the former German possessions over to the Japanese instead of returning them to China, was protested. On December 9, 1935, an anti-Japanese demonstration marked the beginning of the resistance against Japan. Mao Ze Dong (Mao tse-tung) proclaimed the birth of the People's Republic of China in Tiananmen Square. In 1966 at the beginning of the cultural revolution one million schoolchildren gathered here waving the famous little red book of Mao's sayings.

On the square are located the monuments to the People's Republic: **Mao Ze Dong's Mausoleum**, the **Great Hall of the People** and the **Monument to the People's Heroes**. Visit them, or go on to the Imperial Palace.

Tour 15

● ● ●**The Gu Gong (Imperial Palace** or **Forbidden City)** is open from 8:30 to 16:30, though no entry is allowed after 15:30. the Palace is enormous, covering some 200 acres with various buildings containing 9,000 rooms in all. Some people can rush through this place in an hour and check if off on their list, but it is nearly impossible to get even an idea of it in one day.

A Night at the opera

There are several opera houses, but the most convenient one is on Goldfish Lane a few blocks north of the Beijing Hotel off Wang Fu Jing. The opera costs only a matter of pence if you buy your ticket at the theatre yourself. There are plenty of seats available and even though it begins at 19:00, there is no need to arrive until later. To western ears the singing is piercing and the music loud, so chances are very remote that you will end up staying for the entire performance. Many tour groups will stay no longer than 20 minutes. The plot starts slow and quiet, but thickens as the evening rolls on, until the variety and richness of the costumes and choreography becomes quite exciting to our western eyes.

TOUR 16
BEIJING

After a day of touring on your own, a guided tour makes a relaxing change. Put on your most comfortable walking shoes for a visit to the Great Wall and the Ming Tombs.

Suggested Schedule	
	Breakfast in Beijing.
9:00	Departure.
	Ming Tombs.
	The Great Wall.
Evening	Peking duck dinner.

Sightseeing highlights

●●● **The Great Wall:** When we first visited the Great Wall, we expected to be disappointed. Instead we found one of the most powerful structures ever made by man.

Called by the Chinese the Long Wall of 10,000 Li (Wan li chang cheng), it is actually 12,700 li long (6,350 km or 3,800 miles). Construction began in the 5th century BC in small stretches to protect various areas. The first Qin Emperor (221-207 BC) linked up the pieces to defend the empire from the Xiong nu. It took 300,000 men ten years to finish.

Most tours stop first at the **Ming Tombs** (Shisan Ling, or Thirteen Tombs). Built between 1409 and 1644, they are spread over 40 square kilometres, but only two are presently open to the public. Avoid these. The crowds are horrendous and entering the tombs is like entering a subway made for giants. Most of the objects in the tombs are poor replicas and there is precious little time to pause and study them because of the crowds.

The Sacred Way with 24 stone animals and 12 warriors, the Great Red Gate and the Tablet Pavilion, all above ground, are well worth visiting.

The trip on to the Great Wall, less than an hour, is very high in anticipation. Once you reach the wall itself and climb to the top, go left. The wall is flatter to the right, longer and easier, so that is where the masses go. Not more than half a mile up the hill to the left the wall returns to a heap of rubble. To fully appreciate the dramatic impact you need to get that far. In places the wall will seem almost vertical, with high leg-stretching steps, and you'll need to hang on both going up and coming down. It is worth the effort. Be sure to wear your most practical walking shoes.

Tour 16

The Great Wall

万里长城

BADALING

SHISANLING 明十三陵

CHANGPING

Yongding R.

BEIJING

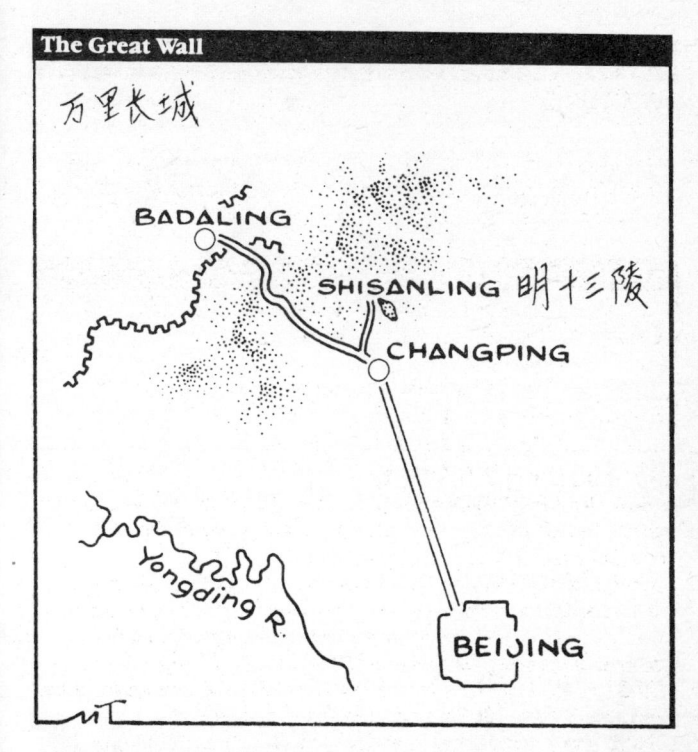

You will get back to Beijing around 17:00 or 18:00, a good hour to go out for a Peking duck dinner.

Guided tours

Most tours combine the Great Wall at Badaling and the nearby Ming Tombs. Tours go down in price from £13 ($20) a person. The most expensive tours leave from the most expensive hotels, and vice versa.

The taxi company operating out of the Qiao Yuan Hotel offers some good tours for this and the other excursions. They depart from the hotel in minibuses around 9:00, or whenever the buses are full and they don't expect any more passengers. These tours are inexpensive and well organised. The itinerary varies, so inquire about the route that a given tour will follow.

In 1986-87 a new section of the Great Wall opened at Mu Tuab Yu. It is more isolated, and most people think it is more dramatic. At the time of writing, tours were not yet going to the new section.

A costly but comfortable solution (under £30 ($50), depending on your bargaining skills and where you book it) is to hire a car and driver for the day through CITS or take a taxi for the day. A sightseeing helicopter flies over the Great Wall and stops at the Ming Tombs. It can be booked at the Holiday Inn Lido.

Visit the Great Wall as early or late as possible in order to avoid the crowds. Late is better, especially in winter when you might get a sunset. Unfortunately it closes at 17:00 pm and no one is allowed to enter after 16:00.

TOUR 17
BEIJING

Today is for wandering, relaxed sightseeing and shopping. The biggest problem will be lugging your purchases with you. Depending on where you are staying, you might stop at your hotel during the day to drop off packages, or go to the post office and post them home. Start at the Yonghegong and Confucius Temple in the northern part of the city and travel south to finish the daylight hours at the Temple of Heaven to visit our favourite silk shop.

Suggested Schedule	
Morning	After breakfast take a taxi to the Yonghegong. Visit the Confucius Temple.
Afternoon	Lunch and shopping. Visit Beihai Park, National Minorities Palace. Taxi to Temple of Heaven. Shopping.
Dinner	Dinner and acrobats.

Half-day tour 1

After breakfast take a taxi to the **Yonghegong** (**Lama Temple** or **Palace of Eternal Harmony** ●). This Tibetan-Mongolian yellow sect temple was built in 1694 as the Imperial residence for Prince Yongzheng. In 1744 it was transformed into a Lama Temple.

The temple has been well restored, but it is more a museum than a place of worship even though there are a few young lamas around. If you have never experienced a Tibetan temple this is an excellent first encounter. If, however, you have spent time in functioning temples in the Himalayas, this one may be disappointing.

Down the street and around the corner is the **Confucius Temple** ● used for the worship of Confucian disciples. The ones in Qufu are more impressive, but this is one of the most unfrequented sights in Beijing and is pleasant because of its lack of crowds. It is a nice place to while away an hour or two.

Now there are several pleasant choices to make. If your stomach and legs say it is lunch time, the **Bamboo Gardens Hotel** with its garden restaurant is close enough for lunch. You are also close to the **White Peacock**, a favourite shop for foreigners living in Beijing. The merchandise is varied and of

Central Beijing

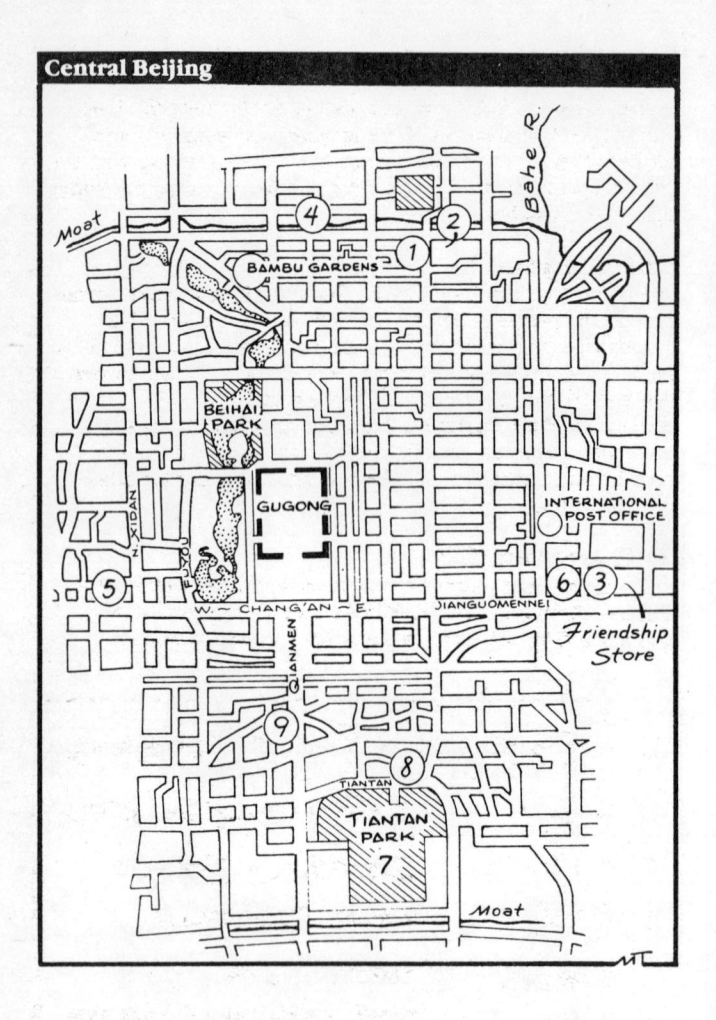

good quality, the prices are the best we have found, and the service is excellent.

Privately owned, the shop offers commissions to the salespeople, giving them the incentive to be hardworking, industrious and alert.

When you are ready to leave either the shop or the Bamboo Gardens you will not have a taxi waiting unless you have thought ahead and got someone to call one for you. They don't cruise in this area.

From here, the general plan is to go from this northern part of the city toward the south, ending the daylight hours at the Temple of Heaven Gates and then visiting our favourite silk shop.

In between lie a wealth of possibilities. Realistically, you will not have time to do all we suggest in one day. Choose what you will, disregard the rest or save it for another day. Here are some logical combinations:

Half-day tour 2
One is the lovely **Beihai (North Sea) Park**. You could wander through the pathways of the Jingxinzhai and see the White Dagoba Hill. This version of the stupa was rebuilt in 1741. Sit in the park for a while studying the Nine Dragon Screen, 16 feet high and 90 feet long made of glazed bricks.

The **Fangshan Restaurant** serves sumptuous banquets; reservations are necessary. There is a pastry shop nearby for more informal snacking. The Beihai Park will make for a few pleasant hours.

Half-day tour 3
If the minority groups interest you, head for the **Nationalities Cultural Palace** next to the **Min Zu Hotel** where you could have a snack in their coffee shop or lunch in their restaurant.

1.	中国国际技术交流中心	CITIC Building
2.	雍和宫	Yonghegong Temple
3.	孔庙	Confucius Temple
4.	白孔雀商店	White Peacock
	北海公园	Beihai Park
5.	民族文化宫	Nationalities Cultural Palace
6.	国际俱乐部	International Club
7.	天坛	Temple of Heaven
8.	顾繡丝绣公司	Yuan Long Embroidery Silk Company
9.	Dazhalan (Acrobatics) Theater	

The museum houses both temporary and permanent exhibits which are interesting and well done. The museum and the hotel gift shops carry books on the minorities and samples of their crafts. This may be the only place in China where these particular items are for sale, so if they interest you buy them now.

Should shopping be your passion, the **Friendship Store** is the next stop. Until recently Friendship Stores were the only places that carried tourist-oriented items, and it is still necessary to go there for certain things. The prices are higher than elsewhere and the service varies from poor to downright rude.

If you have not already discovered the deli and the supermarket on your first day in town, now is the time to do so. Here you can join the inevitable contingent of backpackers in the midst of a feeding frenzy. They have been on the road for months and have cultivated fierce cravings. (If you happen to be a peanut butter addict, the brand in the glass container is better than the plastic one.)

The **International Club**, just next door, is a popular place for the resident foreigners and tourists are welcome for lunch.

By now you might be laden down with purchases and wanting to head for the Post Office to get rid of them. It is a little less than half a mile away, and you can get there on foot. See the section on sending packages in the introduction. The catch is there is another shopping trip scheduled for tonight, but it is mostly for silk goods and their weight and size will allow you to carry them home if you desire.

Half-day tour 4

The **CITIC** building is also in this vicinity; there is some information on it in the restaurant section.

Hopefully we haven't exhausted you yet and you are still up to taking a taxi from the Friendship Store to the **Temple of Heaven● ● ●**. The Temple (Tiantan) is located in a beautiful park which is open from 6:00 to 22:00 during the summer. No entry is allowed after 21:00. (This can also be done conveniently at the end of 'Tour 18'.)

The Temple itself is open from 8:30 to 18:30. This late closing hour offers you two luxuries. One is the possibility of relative solitude, because the Chinese like to eat early and probably won't be around after 17:30, and the second is the late afternoon light, which can be exciting if you are fortunate enough to have a clear day. Not that the temple needs any help. It is majestic and awe inspiring in any light.

First built in the 15th century, it was repaired in subsequent years, particularly in the 18th century under the reign of Qian Long. It was here at the Round Mound that the Emperor at winter solstice reported to the heavens all the important events of the year. In the first month of the year he rendered homage to the heavens to gain their confidence and in later periods to pray for a good harvest. After the establishment of the republic the government tried to continue the tradition.

Now that this moving spiritual experience is behind you, its time to spend more money. Leave the park through the North Gate, cross the street, go right and on the corner is the **Yuan Long Embroidery Silk Company** at 55 Tiantan Road. Open from 9:00 to 19:30, they have a good assortment of western style clothing at reasonable prices. It is a fine place to buy silk shirts and pyjamas. Some of the salespeople are friendly while others behave as if they were working in the Friendship Store.

The taxi station across the street will get you back to your hotel or out to dinner.

One last possibility would be to go and see the acrobats at the **Dazhalan Theatre**, not too far away, for after-dinner entertainment.

TOUR 18
BEIJING

This is a set trip with three destinations, and most tours are the same. The Fragrant Hills, the Temple of the Sleeping Buddha and the Summer Palace.

Suggested Schedule	
	Breakfast at hotel.
9:00	Tour departure for:
	Fragrant Hills Park.
	Temple of the Sleeping Buddha.
Optional:	Temple of Awareness.
	The Summer Palace

Getting there
Make transport arrangements, whether by guided tour or private car and driver, the same way as you did to visit the Great Wall (Tour 16).

Sightseeing highlights
● ● **Fragrant Hills Park (Xiang Shan)**, also called Western Hills Park is your first destination. A 20-minute chair lift goes to the top. A special ticket window is available where, for a small additional charge, you can avoid waiting in the queues. When you get back down from the top, the Fragrant Hills Hotel on this hillside is a popular spot to stop for coffee, and the hotel itself is lovely enough to warrant a visit.

● ● **Temple of the Sleeping Buddha (Wo fo si)** is nearby. Cast in 1331 it is made of 500,000 pounds of copper. The Temple is also known for its rare trees.

● ● **Temple of Awareness (Jueshensi):** A regular tour probably won't get you there, but if you are travelling by private car or taxi this temple, commonly known as the Temple of the Great Bell, is worth visiting. There are 40 different bells in the temple. The largest weighs 46.5 tons and dates from the Ming Dynasty.

● ● ● **The Summer Palace** is your main destination for today. Allow at least a few hours to see the gardens, buildings and lakeside walkways, covering over 700 acres. The palace was built in the 12th century. Over the years it has been subjected to much destruction and rebuilding. As in many areas of Beijing, the Europeans damaged and pilfered the palace in the late 19th century. Most of the present buildings were restored in 1903, but work is still going on. The Marble Boat, for example, was still being worked on when we were there last in the autumn of 1986. Some of the buildings within the grounds have additional entrance fees, and they are usually worthwhile. These special areas have guides dressed in Qing costumes, helping to convey an image of the lifestyle of the time. Most important, they are less crowded, permitting you a more peaceful contemplation.

The tour bus leaves here in time to get you back to your hotel around five. If you haven't been to the Temple of Heavenly Peace yet, this would be a good time since it is open late.

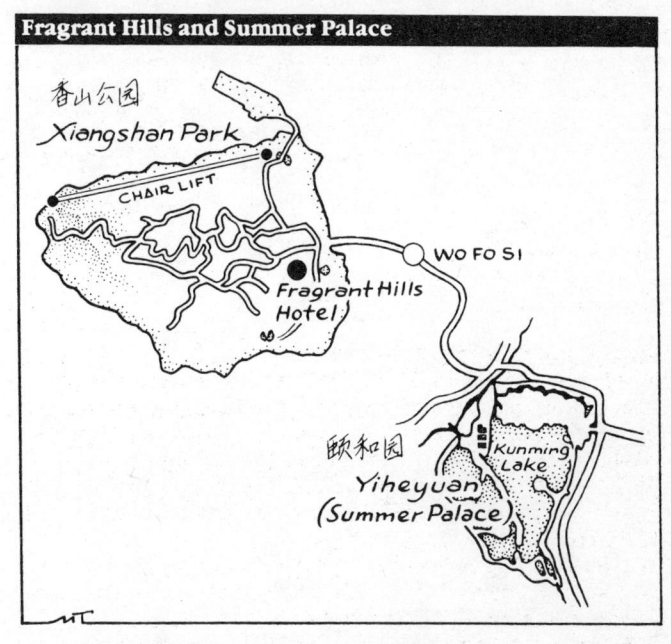

Fragrant Hills and Summer Palace

香山公园
Xiangshan Park
CHAIR LIFT
WO FO SI
Fragrant Hills Hotel
颐和园
Yiheyuan
(Summer Palace)
Kunming Lake

TOURS 19-22
BEIJING — HONG KONG — HOME

Tour 19
This is a 'slack' day to allow flexibility in your itinerary. Skip it to get back on schedule if you took one of the 'Itinerary Option' side trips to Wuyi Shan or Putuo Shan described in Tours 4 and 5, or if you chose to spend an extra day at one of your earlier destinations, or if transport arrangements went haywire somewhere along the way.

If, however, you've followed the main itinerary like clockwork, good for you! You have an extra day to explore Beijing on your own, perhaps doing last-minute shopping or revisiting a sightseeing highlight where you wished you could spend more time. The English Corner meets during the day in the southeast corner of Zizhuyan Park, west of the zoo. (Skip the zoo.)

Tour 20
Depart Beijing for Hong Kong on one of CAAC's morning flights, arriving in Hong Kong in the afternoon. Spend the evening on the town and the night at the YMCA (See 'Tour 1').

If you have more than three weeks to explore China, itinerary options explained at the end of this itinerary present several intriguing possibilities.

Tour 21
Today you will probably awaken to culture shock. Go all the way — head for one of the big hotels for a buffet breakfast or bacon and eggs as you know them. Then tour, shop and eat until bedtime. Here are a few suggestions:

One of the few areas in Hong Kong that retains the atmosphere of times past is **Hollywood Road**, lined with antique shops. To get there, take the Star Ferry across to the Hong Kong side, then take a taxi or a very long, interesting walk past furniture and calligraphy shops on this winding street. If you enjoy a great variety of seafood and don't require elegant surroundings, visit the night open-air market to the left of the Macao Ferry pier, which you can reach by walking downhill from Hollywood Road.

On the Hong Kong side you can take a taxi or the free shuttle bus from the Star Ferry (9:00-19:00) to the **Peak Tram**. At the top is a romantic, though tourist-oriented, restaurant as well as a beautiful view of Hong Kong.

Take a bus to the town of **Stanley** for bargain clothing shopping and a glimpse of the more rural side of Hong Kong.

The receptionist at your hotel will be able to tell you which bus. Just beyond Stanley are the floating boat restaurants of Aberdeen.

If you have time, you can reach the other nearby islands by ferry or take a hydrofoil to Macao.

After dark the **Temple Street Market** appears off Jordan road on the Kowloon side. It is full of stalls with clothing bargains and delectable seafood.

For a short outing, turn left on Salisbury Road from the YMCA and go to the **New World Centre**. Find here an immense dark glass complex filled with every type of shop and restaurant imaginable, including the Beverly Hills Deli.

Tour 22

Depending on your departure time, some shopping and a last dim sum meal might fit into your schedule.

The key to your last day should be relaxation. Don't overdo — it's a long flight home. One last purchase or sight is not worth starting a long flight frazzled.

Leave for the airport early to allow for traffic delays.

A pleasant, un-hassled flight is a wonderful time to review your trip and prepare for your return HOME.

ITINERARY OPTION: XIAN

The best-known tourist spot in China which we have not included in this itinerary is the terra cotta army at Xian, one of the most unusual recent archaeological discoveries anywhere. If you have extra time, you might want to visit Xian as a side trip before returning to Hong Kong. If you have a *lot* of extra time you could continue from there to Chengdu (see 'Adventurers' Option').

Xian (pop. 3m) has the well deserved reputation for being the only significant 'rip off' city in China. Travellers commonly report being lied to, cheated and ripped off by hotel receptionists, taxi drivers, tourist stands and museum entrances; our experience is the same. This is also the only Chinese city where numerous reports circulate of the police arresting and fining foreigners. Xian does not seem to be a place for individuals to travel without a tour guide. Beware of market people whose energy is 100% focused on separating you from your money. They will be loudly hawking everything from £3 ($5) pomegranates to fake — and even real (ie illegal) — antiques poached from the area.

You may disagree with our assessment of Xian, and we sincerely hope that the attitude of the people in Xian toward foreigners changes. When the underground terra cotta army was discovered, many people came here to take advantage of the situation. Many claim it is these opportunists, not the local people, who are obnoxious. There are, in fact, some very nice people in Xian. You may be lucky enough to meet one of them.

Getting there: There are several flights daily from Beijing to Xian, costing about £30 ($50) for the two-hour trip. For the return trip, there are about 10 flights weekly from Xian to Guangzhou, costing roughly £45 ($75), and two 'charter' flights — usually on Thursday and Sunday — direct to Hong Kong for about £85 ($150). (CAAC calls many of their flights to Hong Kong 'charters' to avoid granting landing rights within China to outside airlines.)

Sightseeing: The **Terra Cotta Army** (which the tourist guides like to call the 'find of the century') is impressive, however many people are disappointed with the aircraft hangar environment and poor viewing conditions. Extensive excavation is planned for the next decade. As more is unearthed, and especially as the viewing arrangements are improved, it will be more worth going out of your way to see.

The ruins of a 6,000-year-old village, **Banpo**, are included as a stop on the tour to the terra cotta army. The hot springs called

Itinerary Option

Huaquing Pool, also usually combined into a tour to the army, are uninteresting.

Tours to the army, Banpo, and the hot springs are available from the CITS office at the Renmin Hotel or from the Double Dragon hotel near the bell tower. The CITS tour promises an English-speaking guide to make their twice-as-expensive tour seem more worthwhile. In our case, she only told us what time to be back at the bus. The bus itself was more comfortable. The tour buses stop for lunch at an isolated place, with no competition, serving only set meals that qualify as some of the worst food in China.

Many people find the **Great Mosque** in the centre of Xian, with its traditional Chinese architecture, more appealing than the terra cotta army.

The **city walls** are being rebuilt as an additional tourist attraction. You can expect to pay ten times what a Chinese person would pay to climb to the top.

There is a **provincial museum**.

West of Xian, half an hour by public bus, the town of **Xianyang** has a museum full of 1½-foot-high horses and soldiers so poorly displayed that it's a fast walk-through. There is also a **shadow puppet factory** on the left at No. 40, a couple of hundred yards down the main street beyond the clock tower. They have short puppet plays, then escort you into a showroom where you can buy the same goods that are available all over China.

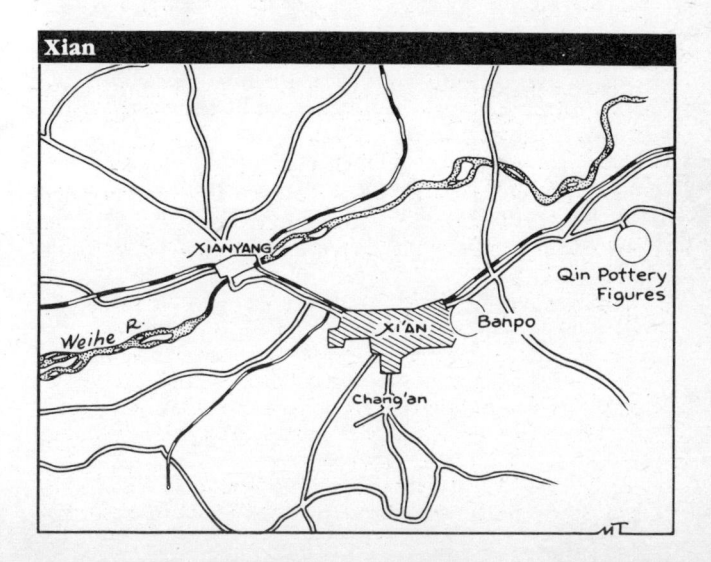

Lodging: The **Renmin Hotel** has adequate rooms at fair prices. However, they will tell you only the most expensive rooms are available. Most of the staff is downright rude.

Double Dragon is a ten-minute journey out of town. The hallways smell as though they have been mopped with urine. Bus service ends early in the day, and taxis cost ten times what the same distance in Beijing would cost.

The **Bell Tower Hotel** is somewhat dilapidated, but it does have cold beer. In Xian in the summer, a cold beer can be very refreshing.

A number of new hotels are coming on the scene, advertising far more than they deliver. We investigated one of the advertised hotels called the **Golden Flower**. The ad promised all sorts of things that no one in the hotel knew anything about. The **Changan**, **Efang Palace**, **Huashan** and **Tangcheng** are all new in 1987. The **Xian Hotel** falls into this category, too, since it only dates from 1982 with a new wing completed in 1986. Don't be surprised if you are charged more than £60 ($100) a day at any of these hotels.

On the way: If you do decide to visit Xian, you might combine it with a trip to Xining, reached on a once-weekly flight from Beijing. Taersi Monastery outside of Xining, one of the best Tibetan monasteries around, is more alive than many of those found in Tibet. From Xining you can come back through Lanzhou and visit their marvellous museum with the famous statue of a flying horse, the Galloping Horse of Gansu. Another Tibetan style monastery is south of Xining at Xiahe.

Be warned though that if you contemplate trips to western areas of China, you'll need considerable time. Transport from Xian and everything to the west of there can be very slow, requiring days to get out. The vast western Chinese back country — the area bounded by Xining, Lhasa, Dali, and Chengdu — is rapidly opening up, however, and it can be one of the most interesting areas for the experienced traveller to explore. For information on this area see *Tibet: A Travel Survival Kit*.

ADVENTURERS' OPTION
SOUTHWESTERN CHINA

Our itinerary takes you to the places in China most foreigners have heard about. It does not cover the entire country. That would be a near-impossible feat in three months, let alone three weeks.

A completely different three-week or month-long tour, exploring the southwestern part of China, is equally feasible. This trip won't take you anywhere near the Great Wall, but rather into remote regions that have only recently opened to foreign tourism. Transport and accommmodation in the southwest tend to be rougher — less comfortable and less predictable. It's for the adventurous traveller only. We describe this trip in detail because it's our favourite. Here you'll find our favourite food, our favourite village, our favourite temple. On this route you can see some of China's most beautiful areas, with favourable weather all year.

Kunming (pop. 2m), known as 'the city of eternal spring', is an excellent base for excursions to see China's colourful minority groups who still live traditionally, with little influence from the outside world. A visit to the enchanting sacred mountain, Emei Shan, a stop-off at Le Shan to see the world's largest Buddha, well-preserved Buddhist cave sculptures at Dazu, surrealistic rock formations at the Stone Forest, China's largest waterfall at Huanguoshu and the captivating scenery along the Li River near Guilin combine to make this an exciting and unforgettable trip.

This trip will introduce you to China's Min Zu or minority people. The Min Zu, 6.3% of China's population or about 67 million in number, encompass 55 different minority groups. Living in the border areas of the south, west and north, these minorities have been less affected by the expansion of Han (majority Chinese) culture. Even today many of these areas show little Han influence.

For an introduction to China's minorities, see 'People of China's Far Provinces' in the March 1984 issue of *National Geographic*.

TRANSPORT TO KUNMING
Direct from Hong Kong: To keep your entry into China as simple as possible, fly direct from Hong Kong to Kunming on one of the twice-weekly flights. The only airline covering this route is CAAC. Your U.K. or Hong Kong travel agent should be able to book it for you, or see the Hong Kong CAAC office. Depending on the season it may be difficult to get tickets at short notice. Be at the airport at least an hour before the 13:40

Southwest China

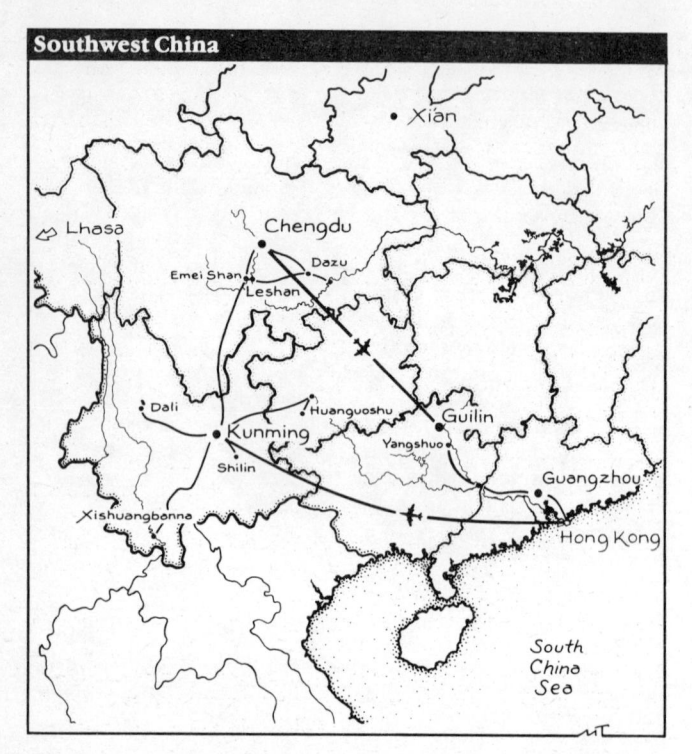

[Map of Southwest China showing Lhasa, Xian, Chengdu, Emei Shan, Dazu, Leshan, Dali, Huanguoshu, Kunming, Guilin, Yangshuo, Shilin, Xishuangbanna, Guangzhou, Hong Kong, and the South China Sea]

departure. Allow 30 extra minutes for traffic jams. If you plan on leaving the vicinity of the Star Ferry by 11.30 in either an airport bus or a taxi, there should be no problem. There is a departure tax at the airport.

Via Guangzhou: Daily flights from Guangzhou (Canton) to Kunming, departing around 8:00 and 18:00, cost about £30 ($50), half as much as the direct fare from Hong Kong. The logistics, however, become more involved. If you take the morning flight, you'll have to stay overnight in Guangzhou and get to the airport early, which is more complicated than it sounds. The afternoon flight is more convenient; you can come in from Hong Kong on either the morning hydrofoil or train and take a few hours to wander around Gaungzhou. This still leaves plenty of time to get to the airport. Allow two to three hours at the airport, since you will encounter many delays.

Taking a train from Guangzhou to Kunming is possible, as is flying to Guilin and taking the train from there. Train routes are very circuitous, going west from Guangzhou though, so this option is impractical for travellers with limited time.

Adventurers' Option

It is more feasible to go up-river to Wuzhou by hydrofoil, then to Yangshou and Guilin by bus, and to fly to Kunming from there. This three-to-four day journey is the cheapest and most interesting route. The area around Yangshou and Guilin is one of the world's greatest scenic highlights — an absolute must on your way into or out of China. See the Guilin option for details.

KUNMING

The baggage claim at the airport in Kunming is the small shed off to the right of the terminal building. Follow the crowd from the plane to where the CAAC bus will be waiting. There is no rush to get on — it waits for everybody. The CAAC bus will go directly to the CAAC office next door to the Kunming Hotel. Just follow the other westerners around the corner and through the gate to the hotel.

Taxis are available at a reasonable cost (agree on the price before leaving the airport if there is no meter). If you have flown directly from Hong Kong you may not have any Chinese money to pay for a taxi. At the Kunming Hotel the money exchange counter will be open and the taxi driver will wait while you change money. (A few Hong Kong dollars set aside for spending money will help in situations like this.)

Lodging: The **Kunming Hotel** on Dongfeng Donglu (tel. 5268 and 2240) has over 1,000 beds in two buildings. One was built by the Russians, and the other is a newer (1979) addition. In 1986, double rooms in the new section went for between £10 ($15) and £15 ($20) a day. The top-floor dormitory (originally designed as a bar) has beds for only a few pounds a night. This building also houses the CITS office, a currency exchange and shops.

The older Russian building, which is gradually being torn down, has sets of two bedrooms with private entrances sharing a common bath between them. The number of beds in each room varies from two to four. In 1986 prices were about £3 ($5) a bed, cheap enough so that if you find a good room you can keep it during your stay in Yunnan and not have to worry about finding another whenever you return to Kunming from the various side trips.

Each building of the Kunming Hotel has its own separate registration desk, and the new section will deny any knowledge of rooms in the old building.

There is a good restaurant in the new building, though it closes early. If you turn up much after 19:30 you'll only be able to get eggs, rice, or a sandwich. This is one of the few restaurants in China where the breakfast of eggs, toast, jam, and butter arrives at approximately the same time and you can expect coffee refills.

Kunming

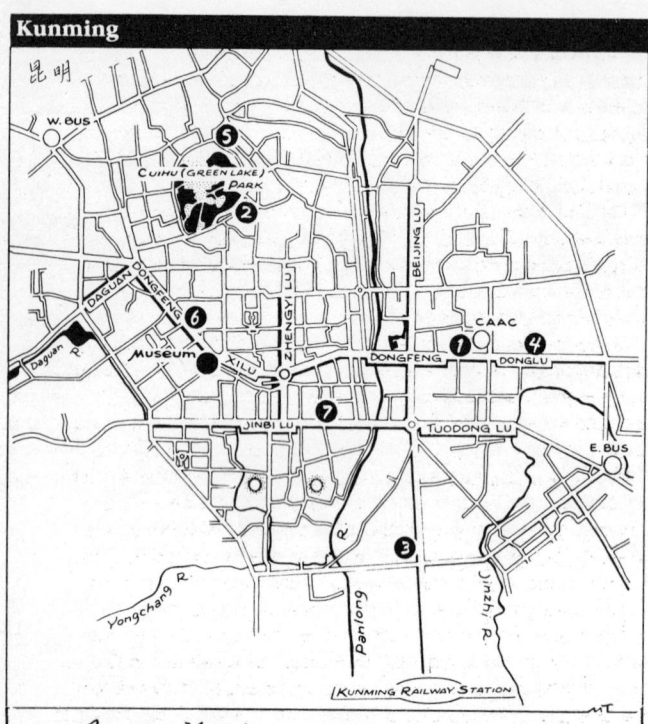

昆明

1.	昆明宾馆	Kunming Hotel
2.	翠湖宾馆	Cui Hu Binguan
3.	昆湖	Kun Hu
4.	山茶宾馆	Three Camelias
5.	潼点厅	Mr. Tong's
6.	红星剧院	Hongxing Theater
7.	咖啡馆	Vietnamese Coffee House

The **Green Lake Hotel,** also known as the CuiHu Binguan, is less conveniently located, at 6 South CuiHu Road (tel 3514). It sits across from an active park area full of interesting evening and weekend activities. If you plan to stay in Kunming and get to know the city instead of taking side trips out of town, this hotel will be a good choice. Prices are around £15 ($20) double. The staff is friendly and the restaurant is good.

The **Kun Hu** near the south railway station is dingy and dirty, has been that way for years and will probably remain so. Financially strapped backpackers stay there. The **Three Camelias Hotel,** a couple of blocks east of the Kunming Hotel, appears to be for Chinese meetings and not for tourists.

Three new hotels are scheduled to open by 1988: the **Sakuna Hotel** opposite the Kunming Hotel, and the **Hai Tau Chun Hotel** and **Sleeping Beauty Hotel** both east of the Kunming Hotel. Reportedly they will be of good quality and less expensive than the Kunming Hotel.

Food: The restaurant situation is continually changing. As in all of China, ask the locals or resident foreigners what restaurants are good. Caution: as private enterprise grew in the mid-1980s, some unqualified people started small restaurants lacking good hygiene. Still, the better small privately-owned places welcome you with a quality of service you'd never find at a government-run restaurant.

Tong's is a good privately owned restaurant located a few blocks north of the Green Lake Hotel. The easiest way to get to Tong's is to get the receptionist to write the name in Chinese, then show it to a taxi driver; taxis are quite inexpensive in this part of China. This hole in the wall has room for four tables inside and, on summer days, one outside. Don't expect gracious dining, but do expect good food and friendly service. Try the fried goat cheese. Order soup whether you want any or not (in China a meal is not considered complete without soup). The candied apples and bananas are sumptuous.

Street eating southwest of the main traffic circle is varied and excellent. A lunch of steamed buns off the street can be followed by coffee and French bread at the Vietnamese coffee shop (see map; don't expect a Parisian cafe). Upstairs is where the foreigners hang out.

Travel arrangements: Begin this rather hectic day by having breakfast at your hotel. Look around for people in the dining room who appear as if they might know the current travel situation.

Make all your transport arrangments for side trips out of Kunming, which may include the Stone Forest, Dali, Xishuangbanna and Huanguoshu. If you choose to take the train to Chengdu, make your reservation as far as Emei Shan at least a week in advance. (See the 'Getting There' paragraphs in the following sections about these destinations.) The CITS office in the lobby of the Kunming Hotel is the place to start. Be there when they open at about 8:00.

There are at least two places to buy tickets to Dali. Check the map in this book and also ask at the CITS office to be sure the locations haven't changed. There may even be new bus lines. Buying tickets to Dali a few days ahead of time should be no problem.

If you want to fly to Xishuangbanna, the people behind the CITS counter may be able to obtain the tickets, but chances are they will tell you to go next door to the CAAC office. If so, the next stop is the main office of CITS, located in room 4102 on the ground floor of the old section of the Kunming Hotel (the '4' in the room number refers to the building). The entrance is at the back. You want tickets to and from Jing Hong (Xishuangbanna) within a certain number of days, as well as return plane and bus connections in Simao. Don't give up! Read the chapter on **Mei you.** As a last resort go to the CAAC office yourself.

The third major trip out of Kunming is to see the waterfalls at Huanguoshu and the Bouyei minority group that lives in the vicinity. The CITS office will be able to help you if you give them a few days advance notice. Otherwise, go to the railway station for a ticket to Anshun.

The last ticket to arrange will be the bus to the Stone Forest. The most comfortable line has its headquarters (which is also a taxi office) within the grounds of the Kunming Hotel, inside the gate and all the way along the wall to your left. The bus leaves from the hotel. There are two additional ticket offices in town on the left side of Dongfeng just west of the main roundabout, but these buses aren't as good, and you must get down there at 7:00 to catch one. The tour companies only sell day return tickets, so if you want to spend the night in Shilin you must buy two return tickets. This presents no great financial hardship since each round trip costs under £2.50 ($4). However, because the tour bus leaves Shilin around 15:00 and gets you back to Kunming around 19:00, a more sensible plan might be to return on a morning public bus.

If you can return from the Stone Forest on an early morning bus and make a connection on the noon train for Emei Shan, you'll save a day. (Check the current timetable.) Otherwise you will have to take a later train or stay overnight in Kunming and take the train the following day.

A walk around town: After lunch, meander toward the main roundabout in town and walk west along Dongfeng to Daguan street. As you approach the roundabout, the tiny side street going west is full of food stalls, tea houses and music in the evening. On the southwest side of this roundabout is a small park. Blind people give massages there, usually on Sundays and sometimes other days. A few feet further on are the alternative ticket offices for Stone Forest trip. A few hundred yards beyond on Dongfeng, give the local museum a quick look. The Hongxing Theatre, further up and across the street, has frequent night-time entertainment for tour groups. Reservations are not needed.

A mile or so farther west on Dongfeng is one of the places to buy tickets for the minibus to Dali if you still need to do so.

Daguan Street, off to the left just after the pedestrian overpass, is full of stalls selling almost anything one could imagine. Especially interesting are the components of traditional Chinese medicine, such as exotic tree barks, and animal horns and innards.

If you get tired, you can catch a bus along Dongfeng Street across from the Kunming Hotel. The bus numbers often change, so when leaving the hotel glance at the bus stop to your left and check the number on the bus, which will take you up and down Dongfeng with stops about every half mile.

Evening suggestions: After dinner at Tong's, wander around inside the park at the north end of Green Lake. Frequently there is public dancing and street entertainment. When you are ready to go home, you can get a taxi at the Green Lake Hotel.

If you are staying at or near the Kunming Hotel, walk west along Dongfeng to the main roundabout shown on the map. As previously mentioned, a side street to the west from the southwest corner of this roundabout is full of food stalls and tea houses with local musicians, singing, and generally good camaraderie.

The tour groups in your hotel will probably be bused down to the Hongxing Theatre not far from the roundabout for some stage entertainment. As an independent traveller you can always join this type of activity in China, and sometimes the programmes are enjoyable. Most places where tour groups congregate will have night-time entertainment inside large auditoriums (left over from the Russians), some seating 5,000 people. The programmes are repeated nightly, so don't feel you must see something on your first night in town. Street wandering will probably be more memorable.

Get to bed early — there is little night life. Get up early too. That's when interesting things happen on the streets and in the parks.

DALI

Dali is among the most pleasurable experiences available in China or anywhere in Asia. Its narrow streets, picturesque overhanging wood-trimmed buildings, mountain backdrops and lovely people are reminiscent of some Nepalese towns. Many people moved here from Shanghai to escape the Japanese invasion in the '40s and stayed. It is not uncommon on walks in the mountains outside the town to meet farmers who can speak English and French and know Latin. Absence of an airport or a railway station limits the numbers of tourists, so the few that do come are made to feel welcome.

Good inexpensive food is served at several privately owned restaurants. Ask around. Abundant fish from a nearby lake, along with regional Chinese fare, makes for quite a choice. There is only one hotel, the **Number Two Guesthouse.** (We've never been able to learn what happened to Number One.) The hotel is basic but adequate and doesn't strain the budget. Dali is worth a little discomfort.

The time you spend in this region (Dali, Shapin and Lijiang) will be the most relaxing time you'll have in China.

Getting there: Due to Dali's popularity since it was opened to foreigners in 1984, direct minibuses are now making the eight-hour trip from Kunming, with both morning and evening departures. If your schedule is tight, an overnight bus can save a day each way.

Shapin: About thirty minutes by truck or bus north of Dali, at the end of the lake, is the market town of Shapin. Every Monday throngs of minority people from the surrounding villages gather here for a colourful open air market that looks and feels like a Latin American Indian market. It is well worth arranging your schedule to be here on a Monday.

The road from Dali to Shapin goes through a fertile level plain between the mountains and the lake, with interesting villages along the way. Bicycles are available for hire next to the hotel in Dali.

Mountainside temples: About two-thirds of the way up the mountain flanking Dali, beyond the three towering 6th century pagodas, through the marble quarries, past the old graves scattered on the hillsides, and on up through the pines, you'll find one of the best temple rebuilding projects in China, especially interesting if you appreciate woodworking. A few nibbles in a day pack, a bottle of Great Wall White Wine, a jacket, and you're set to go. The heavy beams of the temple were crafted and carved in the workshops of Dali like a giant jigsaw puzzle, then carried up the mountain and fitted into place without using nails.

On our first trip here, at the Chinese New Year, we heard chanting coming from one of the buildings. It sounded just like Southwest American Indian women. After some exploration we found a dozen tribal women involved in a ritual we couldn't begin to understand. They invited us in, we sat, intrigued, for an hour or so until they finished, then we walked back down the hill with them.

Lijiang — option for the adventurous: Rather than return to Kunming to catch the train for Chengdu, go from Dali north to

Adventurers' Option

Dali

大理

○ ○ ○ Pagodas

↑ • Shapin
• Lijiang

N →

GATE

farmers market

† church

• Hillside Temple
• Graves
• Marble Quarries

Annual Market Area

HOTEL

Cultural Center

LAKE ⇨

Reservoir

GATE

Kunming ↓

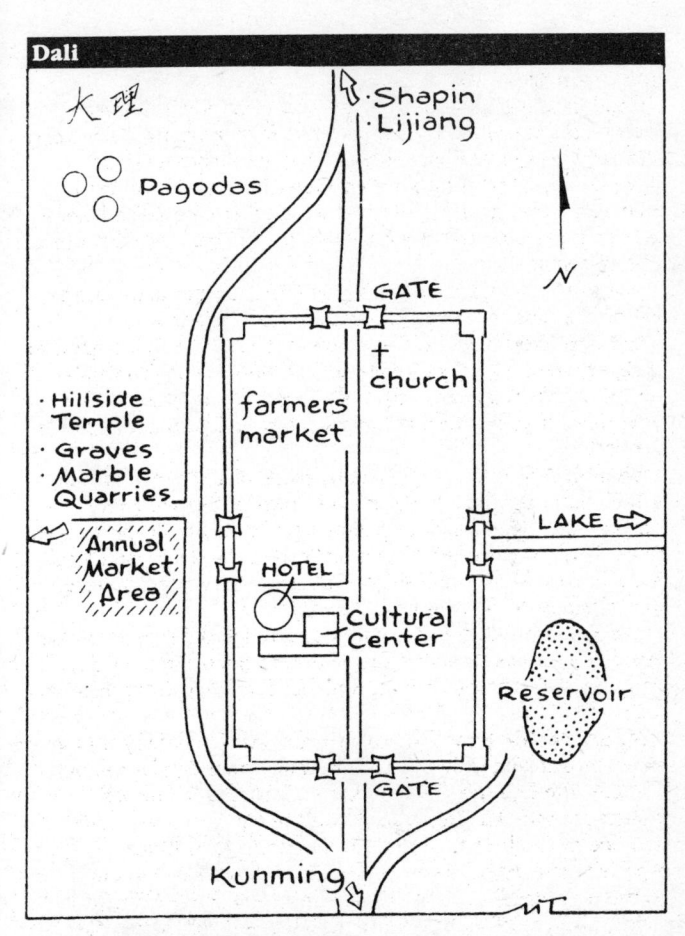

Lijiang by bus. Take another bus east to Dukou, then take the train that originates in neighbouring Jinjiang at 16:40. You'll arrive in Emei Shan at 4:37 the next morning and Chengdu at 7:55. The total trip will take two to three days. The area around Lijiang opened up in 1986 and is just starting to get a trickle of foreigners. This is the home of the Naxi minority. The area has been frequented by botanists for over a century as an ideal collecting area for ferns, mosses, rhododendrons and other delights.

XISHUANGBANNA

Located next to the Burma-Laotian border, the Xishuangbanna region is a popular destination for those interested in minorities. Numerous tribes living along the Mekong river and in the mountains can be visited on day excursions from Jinghong. This area resembles neighbouring Burma, Laos and Thailand more than it does the rest of China. The climate is tropical, with heavy rainfall in early summer and intense summer heat and humidity. During the remainder of the year the weather is superb.

The annual Dragon Boat Festival is the biggest holiday of the year in Jinghong. It attracts throngs from throughout China. The chances of getting there during this holiday are remote, but the event is very exciting if you can somehow make it. The Dragon Boat Festival takes place on June 8, 1989 and May 28, 1990.

Getting there: Jinghong can be one of the more frustrating places to get to and from. There are no direct flights from Kunming. The nearest airport is in Simao, and Jinghong is another half day by bus from there. Since the planes don't fly if there is a cloud in the sky, many people find themselves trapped in Simao trying to get back to Kunming in time to make connecting flights. Arrange your schedule to allow some leeway in case of plane cancellations.

To go all the way by bus from Kunming is a two-and-a-half day trip each way. We don't recommend it.

Flights are scheduled (subject to change) from Kunming to Simao and return as follows: two flights each way on Monday, one on Tuesday, none on Wednesday, two on Thursday, one on Friday, one on Saturday, and none on Sunday. On Sunday and Wednesday the plane flying this route makes a trip to Xian. The surest way of flying is to get tickets for the first flight on a day when two flights are scheduled — at least that gives you two possibilities in the same day. If you are scheduled to fly on Tuesday or Saturday and the plane doesn't go, you'll have at least a two day wait for the next one.

There are no connecting buses in Simao. Both going and coming, unless you are blessed with extraordinary luck, you will be forced to stay overnight in Simao and continue your journey the next morning. For a night each way Simao is okay, though not a place we'd choose to spend a holiday. An alternative some Hong Kong people use, and westerners can copy, is for six to ten people to get together and rent a minibus and driver in Kunming. This could cut travel time in half, and you'd have the convenience of your own minibus in Jinghong. You could keep the same minibus for your visit to the area around Dali. Check with CITS or the ticket office for the minibuses to Dali or Shilin, or the taxi stands, for possible vehicles.

Simao: If you have arranged your tickets through the main CITS office in the old wing of the Kunming Hotel, a car should meet you at the Simao airport and take you to your hotel. The driver is Xiong Chang Fu, the Foreign Affairs Officer, a most friendly and helpful person. The cost of the hotel is around £5

($10) for a double, and Mr. Xiong's charge for picking you up, arranging tickets, etc, is only a few pounds.

Simao has several hotels, most of them basic. The best one is a four-storey white building on the main street with no sign outside. The reception desk is in a dreary dark building in front. The hotel is centrally located with a restaurant in another building at the back. The restaurant's speciality is surprisingly good fried grasshoppers and grubs. The hotel keeps a miserably sad bear in a tiny cage. Nearby on the main street are some fine bakeries, as well as several decent restaurants where you select the food and it is cooked for you. There is also a restaurant of sorts at the airport.

Bring a long book when you go to the airport, as the wait can be interminable.

Jinghong: The only hotel in Jinghong is a group of buildings surrounded by tree-covered grounds. Units in the rear have more peaceful views; none are luxurious. If room choices are available, look them over before choosing. There are better places around town to eat, so don't bother with the hotel restaurant.

As soon as you get settled into the hotel, cross the street, go through the gate and around the stairway behind the left side of the building and upstairs to the CITS office. There, the most helpful, friendly and competent government worker in all of China (her name is Jiang Ya Pin) can arrange anything you need for your stay in this area — even flight reservations from Simao back to Kunming.

Tourist minibuses to surrounding villages are normally scheduled every day. The drivers prefer to drop you off in easily accessible market areas and temples, but if several passengers insist you can get to some really out of the way places. Standard routes are villages toward Mengzhe and toward Damenlong, with their colourful tribal people and open-air markets. It is possible to go on your own by boat down the Mekong River to Menghan and return by bus or boat. The people in the CITS office will be very helpful in explaining available options.

A particularly good restaurant is located along the Manting road, less than a 15-minute walk from the hotel. It is a nationalities restaurant, operated by the Dai people. There is another one in the town centre The CITS office can arrange a banquet of Dai food in a private house next to the restaurant on the Manting road. This will rate as one of the culinary delights of your trip.

The town of Jinghong and the surrounding countryside lend themselves to walking. Well worth a visit are the park and temple further out along the Manting road beyond the restaurant.

A few minutes southeast of town is the Dai village of

Manjinglan. In the other direction, less than two blocks from
the hotel is the morning market. A trip through it may turn
you into a vegetarian for the remainder of your stay in
Jinghong.

Unless other arrangements can be made, you'll need to take
a morning bus from here to Simao, spend the rest of the day
in Simao, then fly on to Kunming the following day. Things
might have changed allowing you to make it all in one day, so
try.

HUANGUOSHU

This waterfall is the largest in China. Other falls in the world
may be more spectacular, but Huanguoshu and the idyllic
surrounding countryside are an excellent place to see the
Bouyei, among the most interesting minority people in
southwestern China. A walk through the fields within a few
miles of the falls is thoroughly enchanting. The Bouyei women,
known for their fine batik work, will invite you into their homes
in hopes of selling fabric and traditional handmade clothing.

Getting there: It's not easy. This area is just opening up to
foreign tourism, and the infrastructure still leaves a lot to be
desired. From Kunming, the only feasible way is to take a train
to Anshun and then a bus to Huanguoshu. Two trains leave
Kunming daily; the best connecting time is on the one that
departs at 20:20 and arrives in Anshun at 8:28 the next
morning. In Anshun you can get a bus and be in Huanguoshu
by noon. As you leave the Anshun railway station, the bus
station is a five to ten minute walk straight ahead (north).
Should you need to spend the night in Anshun, the three-
storey hotel across the street from the bus station has a
modern annex at the back. No signs in English are evident
from the street. There is also a much nicer hotel, the
Kungshan, in a better part of town.

Trains depart from Anshun returning to Kunming at 18:00
and 22:04, both arriving the following morning. The difficult
part is getting a sleeper each way on the train.

It is possible to go from Kunming to Huanguoshu, or vice
versa, by bus. On the map it appears to be a half-day trip
through remote countryside; in reality, it is an exhausting two-
day trip. When we did it in 1986 we had to stay overnight in
Pan Xian; local people paraded us around town and treated us
as honoured guests, but the only room available was of very
poor quality. For that reason we recommend avoiding the bus
until some kind of hotel gets built in Pan Xian.

Huanguoshu: There are two hotels in town, and the only
restaurants are in the hotels. The restaurants serve early, and
you must let them know ahead of time if you want to eat

Adventurers' Option

there. You will find the newer hotel, the **Tian Xing**, just as you enter town before you cross the bridge. The older hotel, the **Huanguoshu Guest House,** is situated in a park around the curve on the other side of the town. Here you get a dramatic view of the falls, and the rooms are attractive and clean. The Huanguoshu Guest House suffers, however, from the roaring of the falls and the smell of dampness. Prices for either hotel are less than £6 ($10) a double.

Spend the first afternoon gazing and exploring the meandering paths below the falls. A descent into the gorge to the other falls is worth the effort.

The next morning check out of the hotel, leaving your luggage at the desk, and head off with a daybag with some lunch. Walk out of town alongside the paved road for about half a mile in the direction of Anshun and look for a trail off to the left, which will lead you to the village of Shi Tou. (Any trail you may find will eventually lead to this or other Bouyei villages two or three miles to the west.) The countryside is a magical Hobbitland and the people are friendly. Have a good walk, and make sure you get back in plenty of time to catch a bus back to Anshun.

SHILIN

Upon returning to Kunming from Dali, Huanguoshu and/or Jinghong, chances are you will arrive in the afternoon. Check back into your hotel and take a long hot shower. The next morning the bus departs for the Stone Forest at 7:00, so you need to be up and out early.

Shilin, which attracts hundreds of people daily, is a well-known tourist sight because it is accessible, interesting and photogenic. The several hundred acres of the Stone Forest were formed 270 million years ago as eroding streams ate into limestone to create imposing sculptures as tall as fifty feet. Between the hours of 11:00 and 15:00 busloads of tourists descend upon this lovely spot, transforming it into a place to observe tourists. The sun overhead causes the geological formations to lose their dramatic shadows. If at all possible, plan on staying overnight. Special Events: June 23-25 is the Torch Festival. The Sani people celebrate with three days of singing, dancing, and game playing in the forest.

Lodging: The **Stone Forest Guest House** is comfortable, convenient and reasonable. Some of the staff members speak English and are helpful. In the evening Sani minority dancers usually perform. The hotel restaurant is passable, and reservations are probably necessary as they serve set meals. There are also many private restaurants in the vicinity.

Tour buses arrive around 11:00. If you are staying

overnight, first check into your hotel. The bus from the Kunming Hotel goes directly to the Stone Forest Guesthouse in Shilin. Upon arrival, find out when and where the public buses leave for your return to Kunming if you plan to get back before 19:00, when the next day's tour buses return. You might also keep an eye out for someone returning to Kunming in a private vehicle.

Walk along the lake where the local Sani women are selling their embroidery work, then enter the Stone Forest itself. The formations will be many times more fantastic later as the sun begins to set and the colours, shadows and light patterns play upon them, but the Chinese tourists posing in hired costumes provide one of the most hilarious sights in all of China. The costume hire area is located at what the tourist map of the Stone Forest calls the 'open stage'. Take your camera.

After lunch, walk around to the village on the opposite side of the small lake where the Sani people live. Handsome, smiling faces will greet you and perhaps even invite you into their adobe homes hung with chili and corn, crowned with drying pumpkins, to entice you to buy their colourful stitchery.

Plan an early dinner, leaving late afternoon and sunset available to explore the Stone Forest at its most magical time, after the crowds have left. Then go back to the hotel, watch the dancing if there is a performance, and go to bed.

Get up early the next morning and watch the sunrise in the Stone Forest. Then go back to your room and check out if you plan to catch the 7:00 public bus back to Kunming. If you are taking a regular tour bus back to Kunming, you have all day to spend here.

KUNMING DEPARTURE

There are two ways of getting from Kunming to Chengdu: by train or plane. The two-hour flight is scheduled daily except Sunday. Allow a full day if you fly, for nothing else gets done on any day that involves flying CAAC. The cost is about £20 ($30). All flights are in the afternoon.

Most people choose to leave Kunming by train, which makes it possible to stop at Emei Shan en route. It is a comfortable trip through untouristed countryside so rugged that the frequent tunnels make it hard to read a book. The glimpses of minority people from the train window seem right out of *National Geographic*. For the best arrival times, take the train leaving Kunming at 11:50, arriving in Emei Shan at 6:37 the next morning and Chengdu at 9:23. Another train to Emei Shan leaves Kunming at 18:35, which would allow you to return from the Stone Forest and catch the train the same evening. It arrives in Emei Shan at 15:53.

Plan on arriving at the railway station at least an hour before departure. There is so much building going on that it can frequently take 20 minutes just to crawl through construction at the station. The confusion is no problem if you have plenty of time, but it is very frustrating when you're dashing for a train. Remember, as a foreigner you can wait in the soft class waiting room no matter what class you are travelling. Eat dinner on the train and go to bed. Train personnel will awaken you in ample time for the arrival at Emei Shan.

Hint: Beware of last minute shopping. The trip north through Emei Shan and Leshan will be easier with little to carry. If you buy an item planning to post it home, allow at least a couple of hours at the post office.

EMEI SHAN

The train arrives at Emei station about 6.:37 in the morning ('Emei' is the name of the town and 'Shan' means mountain, so Emei Shan is the name of the mountain.) Buses will be waiting to meet passengers for Baguo Village, which is where you want to go. Baguo Village is nestled at the foot of the mountain about 10 kilometres from the station.

The **Hongzhushan Hotel** (also known as The Red Candle or Red Pearl Mountain) is a complex of sprawling buildings around a lake. It's tempting to stop here and check into a room. We suggest you continue on and check into accommodation at one of the monasteries in the vicinity. They have more character and atmosphere, and if you don't mind primitive living quarters it will enhance your experience of the sacred mountain. **Baguosi** is the nearest and most accessible monastery. **Fuhusi**, about a kilometre up the trail, is not strenuous to reach and is one of the most appealing. Maps showing local monasteries are available in the lobby of the Red Pearl Mountain Hotel, and if you are overloaded with baggage (heaven forbid), leave it at the hotel while you look around.

Check into your chosen hotel, eat, get oriented and, depending on the weather, plan your day's activities. A good four or five hour sightseeing plan is to walk on up the trail as far as Qingyin Pavilion, where you can get a bus back down to Baguo.

If you plan to climb the mountain and be on top for the sunrise, check excess baggage in at the Hongzhushan Hotel and start on up. Plan on at least two full days for the round trip. The more time you have to stop along the way, the more meaningful the climb will be. If you prefer, you can take a bus or Land Rover part way and start the climb from there. In winter the steps on the upper part of ,the mountain become

Emei Shan

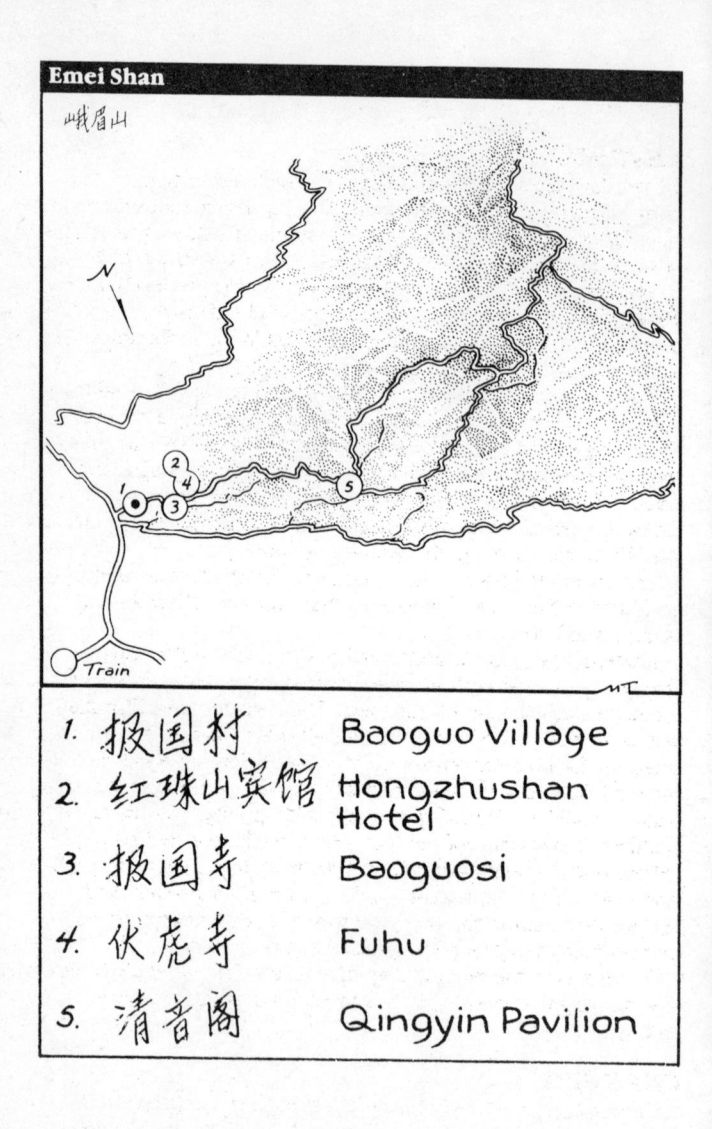

峨眉山

1. 报国村 — Baoguo Village
2. 红珠山宾馆 — Hongzhushan Hotel
3. 报国寺 — Baoguosi
4. 伏虎寺 — Fuhu
5. 清音阁 — Qingyin Pavilion

treacherously ice covered. There is no need to try to get this high up for beauty and spiritual experience; a day on the lower half is one of bliss and tranquillity. Chances are you will be content to wander from one monastery to another having tea and contemplating the serene scenery. (That is, unless it is midsummer when hoards of Chinese tourists descend on sacred mountains during holidays.) *China: A Survival Kit* has more information on this mountain.

LESHAN

Buses leave Baguo for Leshan approximately every hour beginning at 7:00 in the morning. The trip takes about an hour. When you arrive in Leshan, cross the street, walk east to what is obviously a public bus stop and take a bus to the end of the line. If you plan to stay overnight, go to the **Jiazhou Hotel** where you can book a room and make dinner reservations. Another interesting hotel possibility is the guest house within the Dafu temple.

If you've decided not to spend the night here and it is still early in the morning, go to the ferry stop for the boat to see Dafu, the world's largest Buddha. Afterwards, get back to the long distance bus station, where you've left your luggage, and catch the 13:00 bus to Chengdu. If you miss the bus to Chengdu you can take a bus back to Emei and get a seat on the 16:00 train arriving in Chengdu at 19:21.

You could also take a bus to visit the Buddhist caves and sculpture at Dazu from here rather than go into Chengdu and back out to Dazu.

Leshan: Dafu, the Grand Buddha (the prefix 'Da' means large or grand), is such an awe inspiring sight that it is easy to ignore everything else in this town. The seventy-metre Buddha was started in 713 AD and finished 90 years later as a protector for boatmen on the raging river below. To appreciate fully the Buddha's grandeur, take the time to climb from his head down to his feet. Perhaps pose for a photograph on the Buddha's famous big toenail, described in Chinese tourist literature as big enough for six people to have a picnic on. There are other temples and gardens on the hill behind Dafu and on the island in the river. The views from the river cruise give a different perspective of this immense project.

Eat dinner at the hotel and spend the evening wandering the streets. Meander around the nearby markets where the rivers join.

CHENGDU

Depart Leshan on an early bus to arrive in Chengdu (pop. 4m) around noon after a four-hour journey. Most of the hotels are in the vicinity of the centrally located **Jinjiang Hotel.** Chances are your bus from Leshan will arrive at a large new terminal in the south-eastern part of Chengdu not too far from the hotels. Auto-rickshaws in front of the bus station will take you to your hotel for a small price (agree on the fare before you get in).

Leshan

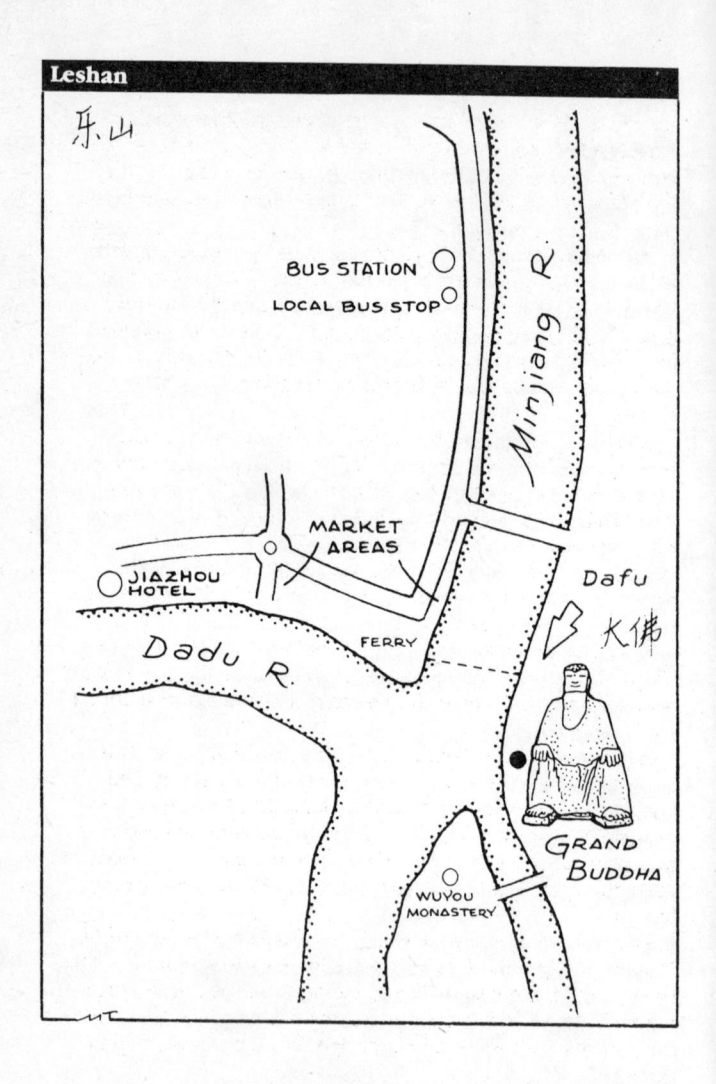

乐山

[Map showing Leshan with Minjiang R., Dadu R., Bus Station, Local Bus Stop, Market Areas, Jiazhou Hotel, Ferry, Dafu 大佛, Wuyou Monastery, and Grand Buddha]

Chengdu is blessed with excellent food, gracious people, fascinating historic sites, relaxing parks and teahouses. This city makes you feel welcome.

There are numerous side trip possibilities. Tibet, for instance, is only a two-hour flight away (see the 'Lhasa' section for details). You'll want to see the Buddhist cave sculpture at Dazu. The nature reserve of Jiuzhaigou is very popular with Hong Kongers who get eight or ten people together and charter a minibus for a week, though as of 1986 this area was officially off-limits to westerners. (When a place in China is closed, it is usually because the Chinese government considers facilities inadequate to accommodate westerners. If a better hotel is built the area will soon open as a prime destination for the travellers with a little extra time and the desire to see remote country.)

A one-day excursion to Guanxian to visit the Dujiangyan Irrigation Project can be organized by the CITS office in the back of the Jinjiang Hotel. The project, begun in the 3rd century BC, is still being used. Nearby Qingcheng Mountain, a favourite of some long-time foreign residents in Chengdu, has the flavour and appeal of Emei Shan without the summer hordes.

Qingcheng is one of the cradles of Taoism, and tourist brochures delight in calling it 'the most tranquil place under heaven'. You can take the trip either through CITS or on your own. Take a bus from Ximen bus depot in Chengdu to Two Kings Temple, explore the mountain, come back by the irrigation project, and get a bus home from Guanxian. Be aware that going by public bus instead of on a CITS tour can make this a long trip.

A shorter excursion is to one of the few zoos worth seeing in China. Take Bus No.9, or the excursion bus to Guanxian which also passes by the zoo. 9:00 (feeding time) is the best time to see the pandas.

A pleasant visit to Wenshu monastery, tucked away down an alley, combines nicely with lunch of Mapo dofu at the well-known **Pock-marked Grandma's Bean Curd** or other similar places just north of the town centre. If you aren't accustomed to a blow-torch on the tongue, you'd better wave off the last spoonful of ground Sichuan pepper they offer to sprinkle on top.

The bamboo gardens at Wangjiang Pavilion, the Temple of Marquis Wu, and the Provincial Museum, each worth visiting if time permits, are easy to reach by bicycle or pedicab. Three other sights—Du Fu's thatched cottage, Qingyang Palace and the People's Park—are all connected into the 'Chengdu Tour' below.

In Chengdu, English Corner meetings take place on Sundays around nightfall in a small park alongside the river, diagonally across the intersection from the Jinjiang Hotel. Ask one of the English speakers at the reception desk for the meeting time. This is an excellent opportunity to meet Chinese people, and they in turn welcome the opportunity to meet you.

First afternoon: As always, the first thing to do upon arrival in a new city is to make transport arrangements for leaving. If

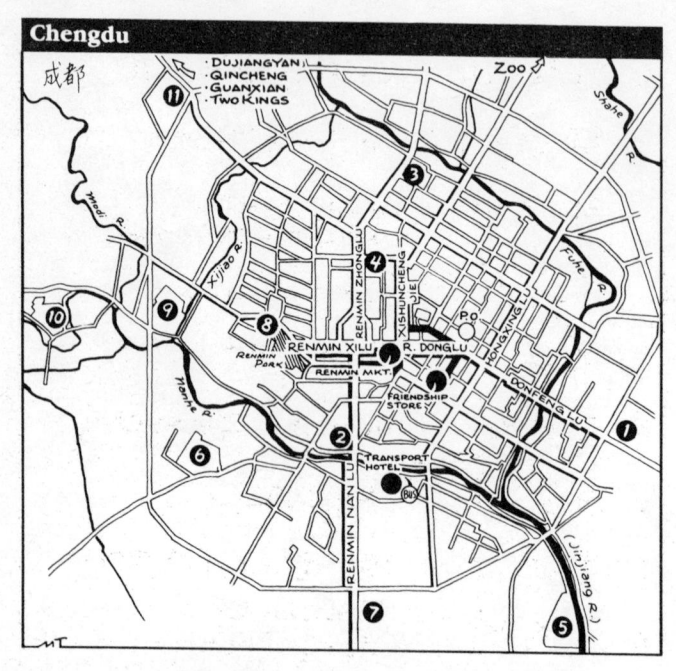

you already have your tickets and reservation for the direct
'unscheduled' Saturday morning Chengdu/Hong Kong flight
(CAAC makes flights unscheduled as a way to avoid granting
landing rights within China to out an outside airline), you are
set. Otherwise you can get a ticket to either Guangzhou or
Guilin. See the options section for details. The CITS office in
the back of the hotel might help you get your plane tickets this
far in advance — give them a try. Also talk with them about
local tours that might be available. If you have to go to the
CAAC office, it is across the street from the Jinjiang Hotel.

Lodging: The **Jinjiang Hotel** at 180 Renmin Nan Lu (tel
24481) is the old standby. A number of older rooms with
baths down the hall fall in the category of 'three bed
dormitories'. These are actually rooms with three beds, for
about £4 ($6) a bed. Renovated rooms with private bath are
around £15 ($25) a double. A recent major renovation
eliminated a lot of the good qualities and replaced them with
superficial glitz: the nice old furniture has been replaced with
'motel modern', the lobby is terrifyingly noisy and glossy, and
the staff is undertrained. It is still head and shoulders above
the **Chengdu Hotel** way out in Dongfeng Lu. Built in 1984, it
has already fallen apart but still charges £10-£15 ($20-$25) a

1.	成都饭店	Chengdu Hotel
2.	锦江宾馆	Jinjiang Hotel
	都江堰	Dujiangyan Irrigation Project
	青城山	Qincheng Mtn.
	灌县	Guanxian
3.	文殊院	Wenshu Monastery
4.	麻婆豆腐	Mapo Dofu
5.	望江楼	Wangjiang Pavilion
6.	武侯祠	Temple of Marquis Wu
7.	省博物馆	Provincial Museum
	人民公园	Renmin Park
8.	努力餐馆	Lu Li Restaurant
9.	青羊宫	Qingyang Palace
10.	杜甫草堂	Dufu's Cottage
11.	西门汽车站	Ximen Bus Depot
	二王庙	Two Kings Temple
	动物园	the Zoo

double. The **Transport Hotel** and the **Black Coffee Hotel,** both backpackers' hotels, are within easy walking distance of the Jinjiang. Neither meets more than basic shelter requirements. A new hotel was planned across the street from the Jinjiang and should be ready for occupancy from 1988.

Food: The food in Chengdu is excellent. Unlike other aspects of the Jinjiang Hotel, the restaurant has actually got better in the last couple of years. The soup poured over the crisp fried rice is our Chengdu favourite.

Alas, the restaurants in Chengdu seem to deteriorate as soon as they become popular. Ask around for suggestions from any permanent-looking foreigners you happen to meet. You might try the restaurant directly across the street from the Jinjiang.The Lu Li restaurant has been around for decades and is still unknown to tourists.

After settling in and arranging transport, there won't be much time left to do anything more than browse along Renmin Nan Lu, the street that runs in front of the Jinjiang Hotel. Head down toward the Mao statue. If it is close to evening and the weather is nice, artwork will be exhibited along the left side of the street. Behind the Mao statue is a large department store where you should spend a few hours sometime during your visit. Only one section, on an upper floor, is now reserved for foreigners. Here they display a modest assortment of antiques hoping to sell them as souvenirs. The rest of the building is crammed with Chinese goods for the Chinese. Another interesting area for browsing is Renmin market. Leave Mao's statue behind, go a block towards the hotel and turn left up the street. The market is to the left before the next road.

Have dinner early. Remember, many restaurants shut their doors before foreigners even begin to think about eating.

Night: Stroll along Renmin Nan Lu to view the artwork. If it is not yet dark, head across the bridge. A couple of hundred yards on your left you will pass the gate to the Sichuan Medical College. Say hello to the guard at the gate, then go in and look around at one of China's prettiest campuses. Between the gate and the Jinjiang Hotel is a side street with one of the more interesting food markets you'll have the opportunity to visit. There won't be anything happening at this hour, so plan on returning early in the morning.

Getting around: Hire a bike and get out there with the locals. The traffic in Chengdu isn't crushing, and none of the distances are great. Another possibility is to hire a rickshaw or taxi for the day. If you do, as always, be sure to establish the price before you leave. There'll be room for haggling. The third option is to use a combination of feet, buses, and bicycle rickshaws.

Adventurers' Option

Chengdu tour: Set off for the Renmin Park. It would be a 15 minute nonstop walk, but you'll be stopping along the way to look at the many places that will catch your fancy, including the markets that flank the park itself.

The Renmin (People's) Park in Chengdu is one of the loveliest we found in China for a morning stroll. There are meandering paths, cosy and private (by Chinese standards) corners, and canals where hired boats shaped like waterfowl float by. But best of all, there is the kind of teahouse you imagined you'd find in China. In view of the lake, under large shade trees and pergolas, are low bamboo tables and chairs. Buy yourself something to eat and a lidded cup containing tea leaves. When you sit down someone will fill your cup with hot water as often as you wish. You can spend several hours relaxing, chatting with the various people who approach you and eating what amounts to a light lunch.

When you leave, go out of the main gate and turn left. At the northwest corner of the park grounds on Jin He Jie street near the intersection with Xiao Nan Jie street is the **Lu Li Restaurant**. Note its location so you can have dinner there. You might make a reservation for the evening. Buses No.3, No.4 and No.5 stop in front of the restaurant, but going west (the direction you want to go) there is only one more stop before they turn around. It is only a fifteen-minute walk to Qingyang Palace.

This Taoist Temple from the Tang Dynasty, unlike most temples in China, is not just a tourist attraction but rather a living temple serviced by monks and nuns. Gongs beat in rhythm to the worshippers' prayers. Voices chant. Smells of candles, incense, and burning paper fill the air, making you feel as if you'd walked into a time warp. In the temple grounds there's a teahouse, and another outside the gates across the street from where you entered.

At this intersection are rickshaws which you can pick up for the rest of the day. From here it is a 15-minute rickshaw ride through pleasant semi-rural back streets to our next stop. Du Fu's Cottage (Cao Tang) is where the great poet Du Fu (712-770) worked for the three years after AD 759. Situated outside the town walls, the cottage itself and the exhibits are not particularly inspiring, but the buildings and grounds create an atmosphere conducive to meditation or daydreams.

If it's early, return to your hotel (about 15 minutes by rickshaw to the Jinjiang), or you might want to go directly to dinner at the Lu Li Restaurant. 'Lu Li' awkwardly translates 'Working Hard at Eating It All'. Before liberation, the restaurant served as a front for the Communist Party. Many of our older Chinese friends in Chengdu enjoy eating here. The restaurant is frequented almost exclusively by Chinese, and foreigners do not receive any special treatment. The food is good and the decor traditional.

DAZU

The Buddhist grotto art work at Dazu has only been open to tourists since 1982 when a road was built to Chongqing, so it is not as well-known to westerners as other grottoes near Luoyang, Dunhuang and Datong. Inaccessibility saved the phenomenal Buddhist cave carvings and sculptures around Dazu from desecration during the Cultural Revolution, and they remain in excellent condition. More than 50,000 examples dating from the 9th to the 13th centuries are spread through forty sites. Most of them, concentrated at Bei Shan (North Hill) and Bao Ding Shan (Treasure Peak Mountain), are easy to reach. The highlights can be covered in one day.

Getting there: Depart Chengdu at 7:30 for the seven hour train trip. Only hard seat tickets are available, but they will be adequate for this trip. Take the train to You Ting Pu where buses for Dazu will be waiting as you leave the railway station. The not-too-comfortable local public buses arrive in Dazu an hour later, passing through one town and some interesting farm land on the way. The bus station in Dazu was being relocated the last time we were there and will probably end up on the left before you cross the river (see map). Ask for directions to the hotel before you strike off on your own. Expect about a ten minute walk from where the bridge crosses over the river. Go to the second street (which should be closed to vehicles) after crossing the bridge, and turn right. If you look perplexed, people will point you in the right direction.

As soon as you arrive, start arranging your route back out. The train you need to return to Chengdu comes through You Ting Pu at 7:42. You might get travel information at the hotel, but before leaving the bus station try to verify what bus you have to catch in order to meet that train. Sometimes there are direct buses from Dazu to Chengdu; if so they will be the easiest way back.

Another possibility is to go on to Chongqing. Daily direct air conditioned buses stop at your hotel around eight in the morning and get into Chongqing shortly after lunch. If you plan to go down the Yangtze River this is the best way to get there. Chances are very good that most of the year you could leave Dazu one morning and be on the Yangtze the following morning. See the Yangtze River section for details.

Food and lodging: Dazu Binguan, tel 237, has a number of comfortable rooms and one very helpful young

Adventurers' Option

Dazu

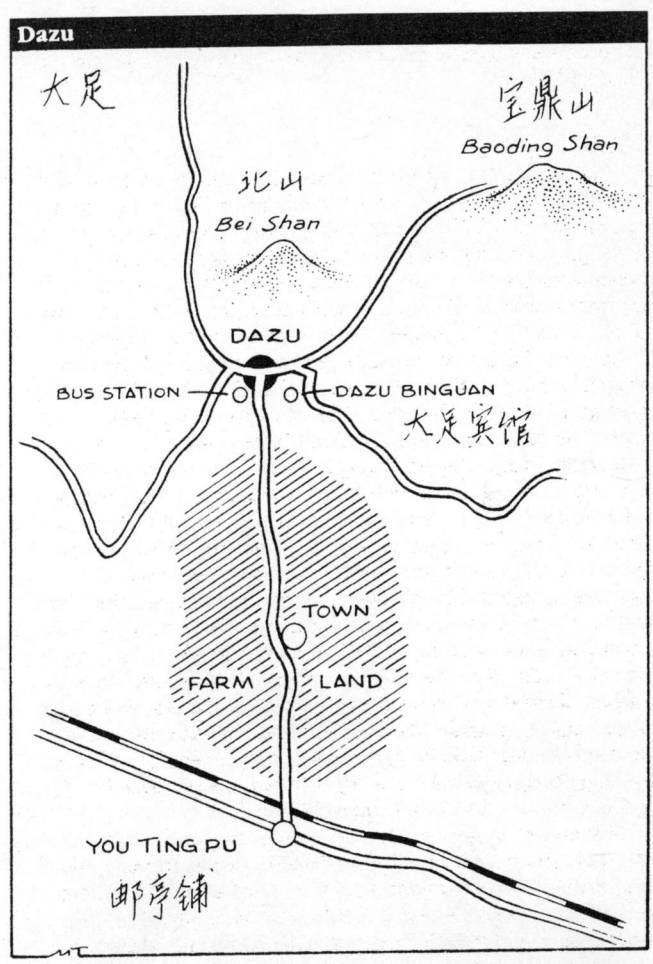

```
大足                           宝鼎山
                              Baoding Shan
              北山
              Bei Shan

              DAZU
BUS STATION —○ ○— DAZU BINGUAN
                              大足宾馆


                TOWN
        FARM         LAND


YOU TING PU
邮亭铺
```

woman working at the reception desk. She speaks English well and can make your life easier if she is on duty when you get there. She or the CITS person in this hotel can arrange local sightseeing and, if you need it, transport on to Chongqing. They might also be able to get you a direct bus back to Chengdu.

Forget about the hotel restaurant with its uninspiring set meals. Instead plan on eating in one of the several small places along the street that have fresh fish swimming in pans in the front. Choose your own fish and point to ingredients in the kitchen to create a tasty meal.

Sightseeing: On the afternoon of arrival, a leisurely 20 minute walk will take you to Bei Shan (North Hill), located (logically enough) on the north edge of town. Compared to Bao Ding these cave sculptures are minor, but they make for a lovely end of the day and sunset spot, set as they are in a park above the town.

After dinner is the time for the promenade. The locals are usually out in the evening and you can enjoy watching each other without the hustle and bustle associated with the big city masses. Dazu affords a rare opportunity to see Chinese life in a small out-of-the-way place relatively unaffected by events in Beijing or the rest of the world.

Bao Ding: There are two ways of getting to Bao Ding, one of which costs about fifty times as much as the other. Taxis and/or guides going from the hotel to Bao Ding charge large amounts and try to rush you through. The best way of getting there is to walk back to the bus station bridge area and take one of the frequent public buses to Bao Ding. You'll want to check the day before to find out departure times.

Several stalls just north of the bridge sell steamed buns which, with a few pieces of fruit, will make a nice breakfast. Toss a few extra pieces of fruit in a bag for later in the day. There are food stands at Bao Ding, but a picnic in the midst of the grotto area will be more enjoyable.

Return buses run about every half hour. As always, check when you arrive to find out departure times. A schedule is posted on one of the food stands, though in fact buses seem to leave whenever the driver wants. As a foreigner, your chances of getting stranded are pretty remote. No one would want to be responsible for having done that to you.

Return to Chengdu: Start early today to catch the train in You Ting Pu at 7:42, arriving in Chengdu at 14:44. Bus No. 16, running from the railway station past the Jinjiang Hotel, is a convenient way of getting back to the hotel area. Be careful on this bus: some foreigners report that their bags have been slashed during the trip.

OPTION: TIBET

The flight from Chengdu to Lhasa last only two hours but takes you a thousand years back in time. Up and out of Chengdu, past the lush foothills, Gongga Shan at 7,556 metres out of the left window, over razor-sharp mountain ridges, the Himalayas to the left, even Everest visible in the distance, the flat Tibetan plateau below...then the plane circles and lands in the forbidden kingdom of Tibet.

Adventurers' Option

Lhasa has improved in the last couple of years. The Tibetan flair seen in much of the building and remodelling now taking place in Lhasa contrasts sharply with the harsh, ugly three-storey cinderblock buildings the Chinese previously erected all over the city. It no longer takes six hours to get from the airport to Lhasa, and sanitary conditions are much better. Transport within Tibet is now feasible.

Buildings such as the Potala and the Jokhang are still phenomenal. A few days spent in Lhasa will whet the appetite for further travel in Tibet. Don't expect to meet the traditional Tibetans that one can find in Nepal, North India or Ladakh. In Lhasa you will find only the remnants of the traditional society after twenty years of tremendous destruction from the Chinese invasion (1959) to the end of the Cultural Revolution (1979).

For any travelling in Tibet beyond a quick hop to Lhasa, the guidebook *Tibet: A Travel Survival Kit* published by Lonely Planet is indispensable.

Getting there: There are two flights daily from Chengdu. The fare is about £70 ($125). It is also possible to take a twice-weekly flight (about 6 hours) from Xian via Golmud to Lhasa. The cost is a little less than £115 ($200).

Lodging: Adequate lower-end hotels can be found for less than £3 ($5) a night. **The Snowlands** remains the travellers' favourite, with the nearby **Banak Shol** gaining popularity. Either place will give you a taste of what it's like to travel at this level—perhaps more of a taste than many fastidious westerners desire.

The alternative is a quality hotel, costing between £30 ($50) and £60 ($100) a night, which won't give any sense of being in Tibet. The newest and best, a joint venture with Holiday Inn, is the **Lhasa Hotel** with 400 rooms. Second choice is the **Tibet Guest House** with 220 beds. A shuttle bus goes from the Lhasa hotel to the city centre charging 2 yuan each way.

Food: Local restaurants offer some basic food. About the most you can hope for is not to starve or get sick. Fuel of any kind is scarce, so food is often cooked in tepid oil over a low fire. Water, which in Lhasa comes from shallow wells, boils at such a low temperature at this 12,000-foot altitude that many germs are not killed. It is better to drink major-brand beer or other beverages, or use a water purifier such as iodine in the water. Remember the altitude and avoid excessive consumption of alcohol. A walk through the meat market near the Jokhang should make a vegetarian out of you for the duration of your stay in Lhasa.

Avoid street stalls and almost everything else there is to eat. It is better to lose a few pounds from not eating than to pick up an illness that can take months or years to get rid of. Many

Lhasa

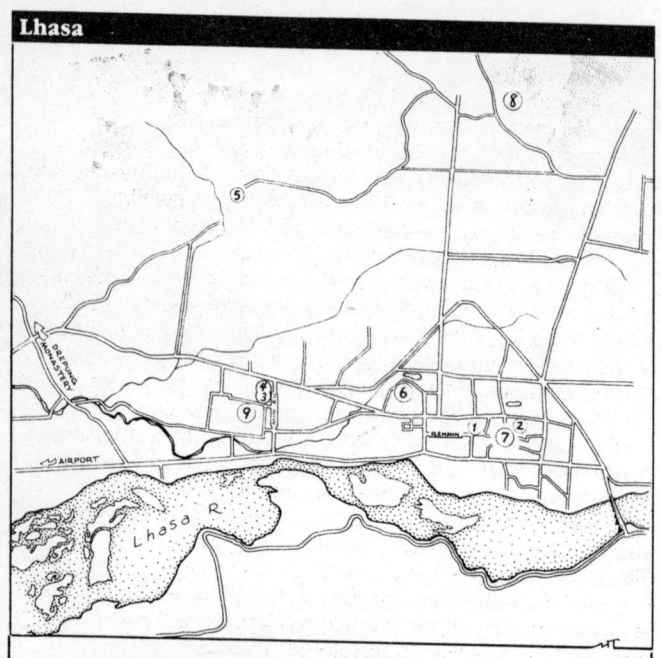

1. Snowlands Hotel
2. Banak Shol Hotel
3. Lhasa Hotel
4. Tibet Guesthouse
5. No. 3 Guesthouse
6. the Potala
7. the Jokhang
8. Sera Monastery
9. Summer Palace (Norbulinka)

Adventurers' Option

travellers make do with yoghurt, canned fruit, and bread which are available locally—not a bad choice. The food at the top end hotels is okay.

Sightseeing: The **Potala** is open Wedesdays and Saturdays only, so plan your sightseeing accordingly. The **Jokhang**, with its many diverse religious pilgrims involved in rituals, is worth many trips at various times during the day and evening to observe the activities. Words cannot possibly describe the atmosphere that permeates the scene. The interior is open during the morning hours.

Besides the Potala and the Jokhang, several other places are worth seeing. The **Sera Monastery**, three kilometres outside town, has some of the prettiest rock walls in Asia, reminiscent of the Anasazi Indian stonework at Chaco Canyon, New Mexico. **Drepung Monastery** can be seen on the hillside to the left on the way into Lhasa from the airport, about 6km outside town. In the same direction, but only about a kilometre beyond the Potala, is the **Summer Palace** (Norbulinka). Just across from the Potala is **Chagpori**, the small hill with the radio mast on top. Close to the bottom of this hill set partially inside a cave, is one of our favourite little temples in all of Tibet. The yak butter statues here are marvellous.

If you have only three days for Lhasa, take a taxi or tour to see these outlying sights. Walking or bicycling without adequate time to adjust to the altitude is unwise.

Winter months can be brutally cold in Tibet. Plan accordingly. In late March the weather is typically mild, in the high 50s. It is not damp and you can expect sun. The wind will pick up in the afternoons and whip dust, germs, and dried fecal matter in swirls through the city. Good sunglasses are important and we prefer glacier glasses to keep grit out of our eyes. Summer and autumn (harvest time) are the most exciting times to be in any rural area.

Leaving Lhasa: A bus departs from the Lhasa Hotel for the airport. The cost is 10 yuan and you should make reservations.

OPTION: YANGTZE RIVER

After weeks or months in central or western China, a four-day boat trip down the Yangtze River is a convenient way to get to Shanghai. Trips down the Yangtze depart from Chongqing. The most interesting section of the trip is through the deep picturesque gorges between Chongqing and Yichang. Many travellers prefer to leave at Yichang where connections are good to other parts of China. Some boats continue downriver to Wuhan, Nanjing and Shanghai. The lower sections of the river are quite uninteresting, with high embankments along the river's edge blocking out most views of the countryside.

The river cruise is a carryover from the era when only large tour groups were allowed into China and they needed activities which could handle 40 people at a time.

About 25 tourist boats leave each week from the Renmin Hotel in Chongqing, carrying forty people each on the four-day cruise to Wuhan. Some are reserved exclusively for tour groups, while others will book individuals on a space available basis. Other boats used by the Chinese for transport up and down the river are not recommended for tourists.

Getting there: Daily early morning flights leave from Chengdu to Chongqing, take about an hour and cost about £15 ($25). The more interesting way of getting there from Chengdu is to take a train as far as the Buddhist caves at Dazu and a direct bus from there to Chongqing. Daily direct flights connect Chongqing with China's other major cities.

At the CITS office in the Renmin Hotel in Chongqing, there are some very nice people who can arrange your boat passage at one or two days' notice. They will also tell you where to go to book passage yourself for the following day. Most boats will allow passengers to spend the night on the boat if they will be leaving the following morning, and a few hours in Chongqing is plenty.

The Renmin (People's) Hotel is almost worth a visit to Chongqing. From afar it resembles a combination of the great domed tourists attractions of Beijing. The dormitories were once dressing rooms for the gigantic domed theatre. The hotel caters to tour groups, not individual travellers, and the food is terrible.

In winter, it is so cold on the river that many travellers have had to spend their entire boat trip huddled in their cabins unable to see anything because of the river fog and freezing weather. It is not a trip for mid-winter.

OPTION: GUILIN

Stretching south from Guilin along the Li River to the town of Yangshuo, you'll find some of the most marvellous scenery ever seen outside a Chinese landscape painting. The area is so magnificent that it is impossible to exaggerate its beauty. The pleasure of this area, beyond seeing it, lies in discovering your very own intimate spots tucked away amidst towering limestone pinnacles, lush bamboo groves and meandering streams.

You can bicycle or stroll on foot, wander here and there, be invited into someone's house for tea, and have some of the most serene times of your life. This area is truly paradise for a painter, poet or romantic.

The city of Guilin has become rather ugly and industrialised. Unfortunately, you may find yourself stuck there overnight. To

Guilin

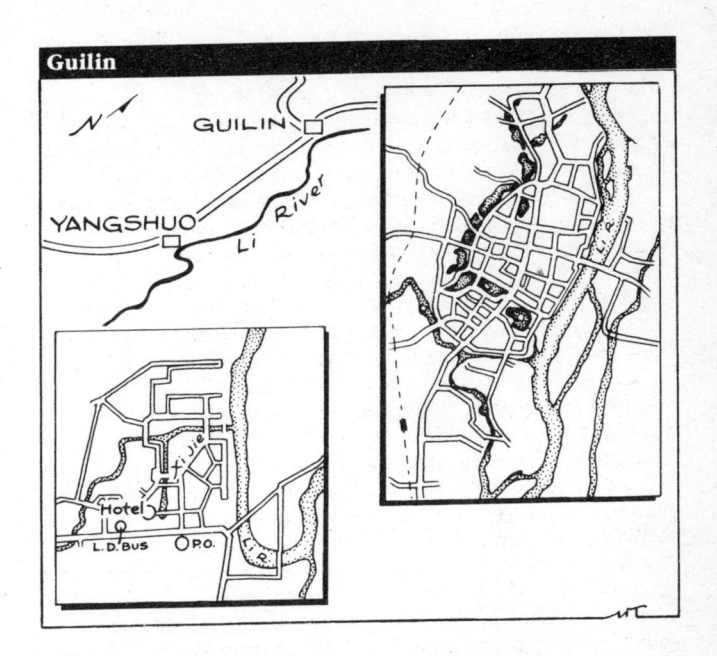

the south, Yangshuo is developing into a stopover for travellers. It has several small hotels and pleasant places to eat. Yangshuo is definitely the place to stay, even though the growing numbers of people doing so are themselves changing the town's uniqueness.

Getting there: There are eight flights a week from Chengdu to Guilin, nine from Beijing and six from Xian. All arrive in the morning after the regular tourist boats have departed down the Li River. Plane fares are about £30 ($50) from Chengdu or Xian and £60 ($100) from Beijing. You can either stay overnight in Guilin and take a boat downriver the following day, or take a bus to Yangshuo the same day you arrive in Guilin. When you leave Yangshuo, a seven-hour bus trip to Wuzhou connects to a hydrofoil going downriver to Guangzhou or Hong Kong. In Yangshuo there will be tickets available which include both the bus and boat. Avoid overnighting in Wuzhou if at all possible.

The total time needed to visit this area is at least two days, most of that being devoted to travel. Three or four days is better, and anything beyond that is luxury. Weather warning: midsummer can be devastatingly hot and humid, winter cold and damp.

The cost of plane tickets from Chengdu, Xian or Beijing, plus your hotel in Yangshuo, meals, local transport and the boat from Wuzhou to Hong Kong will add up to about what a direct flight from any of those three cities to Hong Kong would cost — so if you have the time, this scenic route is essentially free.

Lodging: There are a half dozen comparable hotels in Yangshuo, none very elaborate. The **Good Companion Holiday Inn** and the **Shou Jiang** are both popular. The CITS person in the Shou Jiang, John Lin, is helpful. for these and other hotels, ask and look around when you get there to see which most fits your desires at the time. There are no first class hotels here. The main street leading to the river has several adequate private restaurants.

Sightseeing: Walking, hiking, bicycle riding in the countryside, and short boat trips on the river will fill your time. This is a great area for sketching, photography, journal and postcard writing, and just plain dreaming.

LEAVING CHINA

If you are flying on the 'unscheduled' CAAC flight direct to Hong Kong you will be departing from Chengdu at 8:15 and arriving in Hong Kong at 10:30. The one-way fare is about £70 ($125).

If you are flying to Guangzhou, there are 12 morning flights and four afternoon flights weekly. Chances are you will also be leaving between 6:45 and 10:00 in the morning. The fare to Guangzhou, about two-thirds of the direct Hong Kong price, is the reason money conscious travellers prefer to fly to Guangzhou and from there board a train for Hong Kong.

An alternative to the train from Guangzhou is the 21:00 ferry, which lets you get some sleep in a private room before returning to Hong Kong the next morning. Not many people choose to go by ferry anymore, so they are not crowded and a cabin with two bunks is less than £6 ($10). There is a surprisingly good fish restaurant at the dock in Guangzhou. The ferry is not a luxurious boat, but it fills a need. The book *China: A Travel Survival Kit* contains more information on this trip.

TOURS TO CHINA

There are several tour operators who organise and take groups to China. Some of them do not handle the logistics themselves, but rather, contract through a wholesaler who in turn works through CITS (China International Travel Service) to make the arrangements within China. At one time this was the only way to visit China, but now you can travel independently or choose a tour that suits your interests.

There are tours specialising in birdwatching, Yangtze River gorges, steam railways, photography, camping in Tibet...you name it, somebody offers it. Other groups specialise in setting up educational or specific interest trips to fit any request travellers might make. And there are places which will tailor tours just to fit one person's interest. This is a selection of the main tour operators and travel agents in the UK.

UK China Travel Service Ltd, 24 Cambridge Circus, London WC2H 8HD (tel. (01) 836 9911, telex 263492 UKCTS G).

Kuoni Travel, Kuoni House, Dorking, Surrey (tel. (0306) 885044).

Regent Holidays UK Ltd, 13 Small Street, Bristol BS1 1DE (tel. (0272) 211711).

Voyages Jules Verne, 10 Glentworth Street, London NW1 (tel. (01) 486 8080).

Speedbird Holidays, Alta House, 152 King Street, London W6 0QU (tel. (01) 741 8041).

Occidor Ltd, 10 Broomcroft Road, Bognor Regis, West Sussex PO22 7NJ (tel. (024 369) 2178).

Globepost Travel Services, 324 Kennington Park Road, London SE11 4PD (tel. (01) 587 0303).

SCT-China Travel, Rose Crescent, Cambridge CB2 3LL (tel. (0223) 311103, telex 818822).

Bales Tours, Bales House, Dorking Surrey (tel. (0306) 885991).

Cultural Tours, 64 Pembroke Road, London W8 6NX (tel. (01) 602 3667, telex 8953915).

Travelsphere Ltd, Coventry Road, Market Harborough, Leics LE16 9BZ (tel. (0858) 66211).

China Travel Service & Information Centre, 78 Shaftesbury Avenue, First Floor, London W1V 7DG (tel. (01) 439 8888, telex 262775 CTC G).

China Discovery, 22-23 Denman Street, London W1V 7RJ (tel. (01) 734 9476, telex 8955534 HKITC).

The address of the **China National Tourist Office** in the UK is 4 Glentworth Street, London NW1 (tel. (01) 935 9427, telex 291221), and the UK office of **CAAC** (Civil Aviation Administration of China) is at 41 Grosvenor Gardens, London SW1 (tel. (01) 771 4052, telex 263276 CAAC UK).

Via Hong Kong

Hong Kong Student Travel (tel. 5-414841) 8th floor, Tai Sang Bank Bldg, 130 Des Voeux Road, C. Hong Kong. Either Hattie or Angela at this address can be of great help in planning your trip. They offer a variety of programmes at reasonable rates including train and ferry bookings, Trans-Siberian Railway, group and individual trips into China. This office, the main one, is located on Hong Kong island (which is what the prefix '5' on the phone number means). The Student Travel office in the Star Ferry building on the Kowloon side is handier if you are making your arrangements in person. They will also get your Chinese visa for you. We have received good service from these agents.

A number of other agencies in Hong Kong will handle visas and make some travel arrangements within China. They are **Phoenix Services Agency**, Room 603, Handford House, 221D Nathan Road, Tsimshatsui, Kowloon (tel. 3-7227378). **Trinity Express**, Basement Shop No 15, New World Centre, Salisbury Road, Tsimshatsui, Kowloon (tel. 3-7239761). **Wah Nam Travel**, Room 602, Sino Centre, 582-592 Nathan Road, Kowloon (tel. 3-320367) and **Traveller's Hostel**, 16th Floor, Block A, Chungking Mansions, Nathan Road, Tsimshatsui, Kowloon (tel. 3-687710). All of these places will be able to get visas for you within a day if you turn up on a weekday and are willing to pay around £15 ($20) for special service. One of our friends, F. Tsang, works in the **China Travel Service** office on the Hong Kong side at 77 Queen's Road (tel. 5-236222). They have another office at 27 Nathan Road. China Travel Service is an official arm of the Chinese government but, interestingly enough, the employees work on commissions. They are sometimes more difficult to work with, but they can also do things the others might not be able to arrange.

The main office of **CITS** is 2 East Qiamen Street, Beijing, China. Telex: 20052 CITSB CN. Tel. 75-5340. Contact the sales department and ask for information on their Mini Package Tour Service. They usually deal only with travel agents who have ties with them. The CITS offices in the larger cities in China operate independently, and if you are arranging a tour for a few people it might be worthwhile to get bids from several CITS offices.

USEFUL IDEOGRAMS

在哪儿? Where is ....?
Zai nar...?

我迷路了，请帮我找... I am lost, please help me find ....
Wo ni lu le. Quing bang wo zhao...

我要去... I want to go to ....
Wo/yao qu...

承您帮忙。 You have been a great help.
Cheng nin bang-nang.

您太好了! You are very kind.
Nin tai hau le.

您干吗? Why are you doing that?
Nin ganma?

不方便 It's not convenient.
Bu fang bian.

对不起。 I'm sorry.
Dwei-bu-chi.

请送我到.... Please drive me to ....
Quing song wo dao.

邮局 Post office
You ju

火车站 Railway station
Huache zhan

汽车站 Bus station
Zhong dian zhang

电讯大楼 Telephone, telegraph
Dian hua, dian bao

英语角 English Corner
Ying wu hua hoa ban

机场 Airport
Fei ji chang

Useful Ideograms

北 Bei	North
南 Nan	South
东 Dong	East
西 Xi	West
庙, 寺, 祠 Si	Temple
山 Shan	Mountain
河 He	River
旅馆, 宾馆, 饭店 Fandian, luguan, binguan, zhao dai suo	Hotel
肉馆, 饭馆, 贞厅 Fanguan, fandian	Restaurant
厕所 Canguan, cesuo	Bathroom
公园 Gong yuan	Park
麻婆豆腐	Mapo dofu
家常豆腐 Jiao chang dofu	Home style tofu
锅炮肉片 Guo ba rou pian	Crispy rice
天麻汽锅鸡 Tian na giguoji	Kunming chicken soup

NUMBER GESTURES

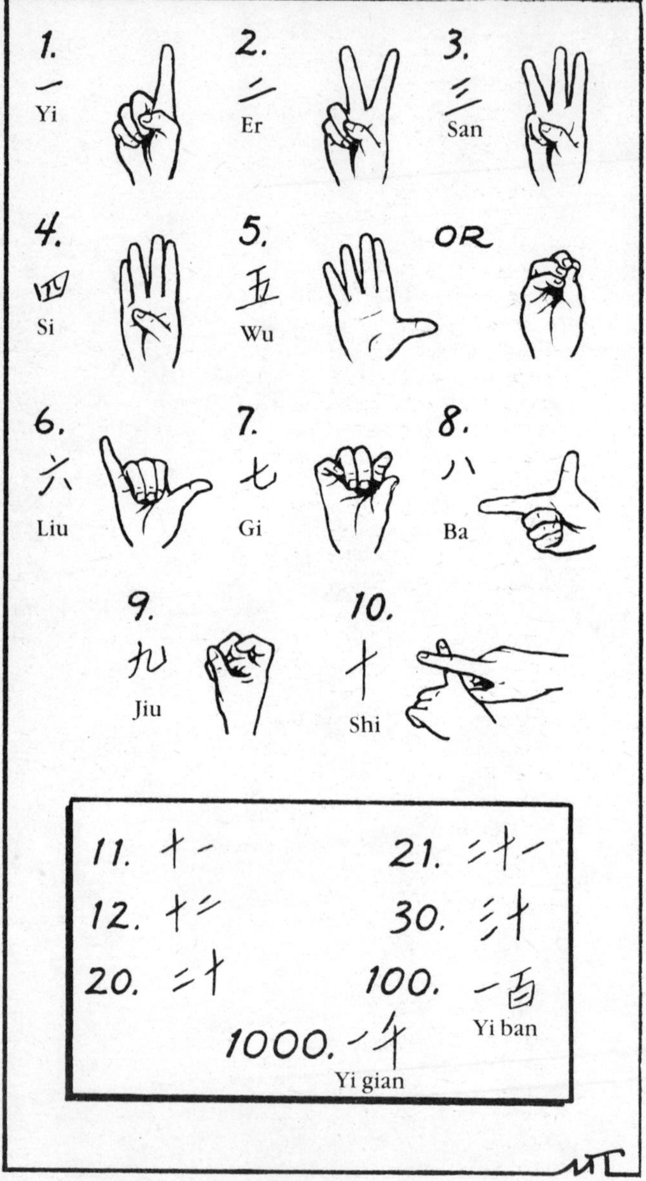

1. 一 Yi

2. 二 Er

3. 三 San

4. 四 Si

5. 五 Wu   OR

6. 六 Liu

7. 七 Gi

8. 八 Ba

9. 九 Jiu

10. 十 Shi

11. 十一
12. 十二
20. 二十
21. 二十一
30. 三十
100. 一百 Yi ban
1000. 一千 Yi gian